A PLACE
OF GRACE:

Find Yours!

DAVID HENDERSON
FOREWORD BY MIKE HUCKABEE

A Place of Grace: Find Yours!
©2021, David Henderson

Foreword by Mike Huckabee,
Former Governor of Arkansas

Cover photography by Michael Weidman

ISBN: 978-1-09835-454-1
ISBN eBook: 978-1-09835-455-8

For my wife, Denise. You have changed my life beyond description.
I am a much better person because of you.
Your smile, your kind words, and your selflessness inspire me every day.

TABLE OF CONTENTS

FOREWORD

"A PLACE OF GRACE"

I've heard the song *Amazing Grace* perhaps over one thousand times, but the first time I heard it sung by the late country legend George Jones, I felt as if I heard for the first time. George Jones didn't sing the lyrics—he lived them, and the depth of his soul translated into his rendition of the familiar gospel hymn. His wife Nancy was the human agent God used to help George truly experience God's grace in a profound and life-changing way.

When George died, Nancy asked me to speak at his funeral. I related that well-known Nashville record producer told me that if ten great artists all sang *Amazing Grace* and George was one of them, it's his version that you'd remember. Real grace is just that. It's not shallow words of affirming that there's a God. It is the depth of a profound encounter with God's forgiveness, His love, and His power.

David Henderson eloquently explains the "Place of Grace" in our lives. Even the greatest heroes of the Bible had glaring flaws and often devastating failures. It was GRACE that restored them, empowered them, and redeemed them.

I've known David for forty years. His faithfulness as a servant of God has been consistent. As he leads you to a deeper understanding of grace, he takes scripture to frame each chapter and uses practical stories and insights to bring home the truth that Jesus is the vehicle of grace that takes us from darkness to life. I pray you find your "Place of Grace."

Mike Huckabee is the host of "Huckabee" on TBN, a Fox News and Western Journal contributor, NY Times best-selling author, and the former Governor of Arkansas.

CHAPTER 1:

Transformed by Grace!

"And suddenly you just know that it's time to start something new and trust the magic of new beginnings."

—Anonymous

John 2:1-11 (NASB)

> On the third day there was a wedding in Cana of Galilee, and the mother of Jesus was there; and both Jesus and His disciples were invited to the wedding. When the wine ran out, the mother of Jesus said to Him, "They have no wine." And Jesus said to her, "Woman, what does that have to do with us? My hour has not yet come. His mother said to the servants, "Whatever He says to you, do it." Now there were six stone waterpots set there for the Jewish custom of purification contained twenty or thirty gallons each. Jesus said to them, "Fill the waterpots with water." So they

filled them up to the brim. And He said to them, "Draw some out now and take it to the headwaiter." So they took it to him. When the headwaiter tasted the water which had become wine, and did not know where it came from (but the servants who had drawn the water knew), the headwaiter called the bridegroom, and said to him, "Every man serves the good wine first, and when the people drank freely, then he serves the poorer wine; but you have kept the good wine until now." This beginning of His signs Jesus did in Cana of Galilee, and manifested His glory, and His disciples believed in Him.

IT'S GOOD WHEN YOU START, TO START AT THE BEGINNING. Before Jesus made his official entrance into public ministry, Jesus performed one miracle. He would then go on to perform nearly forty. It is important to stop and remember what John said, "Jesus did many other things as well. If every one of them were written down, I suppose that even the whole world would not have room for the books that would be written."[1] I'm sure there were many other signs and miracles of which we are simply not aware. This was the first, and it is interesting that he chose to perform this miracle at a wedding. Less than a week has now gone by since Jesus appeared in the desert. John prophesied that Jesus was coming and when he arrived, John said, "Behold the Lamb of God who has come to take away the sins of the world."[2]

There was a system taught in the Old Testament for hundreds of years, that on particular days individuals would bring a sacrifice— often a lamb without blemish. The lamb would then be sacrificed on the altar. Blood would be shed, and man would receive forgiveness. This completed the instruction found in Scripture that says, "Without shedding of blood there is no remission/forgiveness of sins."[3] Now this lamb has arrived and that system from the Old Testament is about to change overnight. Just a few days later, a wedding took place in Cana. We don't know how many guests there were, but Scripture does tell us that Jesus and his mother were there and also his disciples. The Scripture gets right to the point. There was a problem. They had run out of wine, so Mary took the need to Jesus. I suppose that it is difficult to know exactly why she told Jesus. After all, we have no record of any previous miracle Jesus had performed and later in Verse 11, we learn in fact that this was his first. Certainly by this time Mary was fully aware that her son Jesus was the very Son of God himself, so she says, "Hey, Jesus, they don't have any wine." His response captures our attention because it sounds so abrupt. Look at it. "What has this concern of yours to do with me, woman?"[4]

Things are now beginning to change. Their relationship is beginning to change. This is likely the first time Mary asked Jesus for help in a public setting. What Jesus has to say here in the second part, when He says, "what does this have to do with me?" seems to be explained in the last part. "My hour has not yet come." Mary, who is apparently expecting this need to be taken care of, then speaks to the servants and says, "Do whatever he tells you." This is a principle that God's people have attempted to live by for over two thousand years. Read it again.

Do whatever Jesus tells you. Mary knew that Jesus could perform whatever was necessary as long as the servants obeyed. The same is true today.

- Jesus is more than able to do whatever is necessary in your family.

- Jesus is more than able to do whatever is necessary in your personal life.

- Jesus is more than able to do whatever is necessary to heal relationships, to heal people and to heal circumstances.

For the very first time, the public is about to see that in any situation, Jesus the miracle worker can take something that is broken and fix it. He can take something that is old and make it new. Look at what he does. There are six stone jars and each one will hold about twenty gallons—possibly thirty. There are over one hundred-twenty gallons of water available. They are told to take them and fill them to the brim. These pots were used for washing. The Jews had a practice for years that they would not eat until they had washed their hands carefully. We still practice this. "Hey kids, wash up it's time to eat." These large pots were used because they had to wash cooking utensils as well, and the pots and pans.

Mary tells them to fill them and John reports that they filled them to the brim. Now, I am not sure why we have that particular detail, except that it does point out that nothing else was added. No wine was added. No Kool-Aid was added. No food coloring was added. Just water, filled to the top. Jesus chooses some of the servants to help again and he tells them to draw some out and take it to the master of the banquet. Not to the waiters, not to the maître d'... take it to the master. The main guy. These would be very heavy. A gallon of water weighs just over eight pounds so each container may have weighed in excess of two hundred pounds and there were six of them. There were more than just a few men carrying these, as they weigh over a half ton.

The host asked for wine and they brought water. It happens sometimes. "I ordered sweet tea, you know the stuff dripping with sugar. This is unsweetened tea. This is terrible." Or, "I ordered Coke, not Diet Coke." The host ordered wine and they brought water. Of course they were just doing what Mary told them to do. Jesus told them as well, so they were just following orders. We know it was water when they left the kitchen, so we have to conclude that the water became wine between the kitchen and the head table at the banquet. It is like the waiter walking out of the kitchen carrying a whole side of beef and he says, "I need you to become a nice ribeye, medium well by the time we get to the table." That takes faith and obedience. It's difficult to do what God tells us to do when we look at the circumstances. It often looks virtually impossible. As much as we desire to ask so many questions, to dot every "I" and cross every "t" and know every single detail, God says, "Just do what I told you to do." That is what Mary said and what Jesus requested. This is what the master of the banquet, not Jesus—I'm speaking of the Master of Ceremonies—told them to do.

They discussed it with no one and they marched out with it. They took it over to the Master of Ceremonies. Since he was responsible, he had to make sure all the food and drink was acceptable. When he tasted the wine, the Scripture says he did not know from where it had come. The master was obviously surprised because this wine actually tasted better than the wine they had earlier. It was customary to serve the best wine first. Then, when people didn't care as much what it tasted like, you would bring out the lesser wine, the one that was not so good. Just as there is grape juice and wine today, there was intoxicating wine and non-intoxicating wine in that day. The word here in the Greek is *oinos*, and it refers to both so that doesn't help us know which one it was.

Verse 11 reminds us that every miracle Jesus performed had a purpose. It was never simply a display of power. John said Jesus performed this first sign in Cana. What is a sign? When you're traveling down the highway and you see a road sign, that sign is always pointing you toward something that is an important marker. Main

Street. Uneven lines. School zone. Slow down. Curve in the road. Get prepared. Ice on the roads. Trouble is ahead. However, signs are not always negative. If you're traveling down the highway, there are also positive signs. Cracker Barrel ahead. Rest stop ahead.

Several things happened as a result of this miracle:

(1) Jesus revealed His glory. The glory of God was revealed that day.

(2) His disciples put their faith in him—apparently for the first time. Remember, his brother James did not believe until the resurrection. Their faith was solidified at this moment and now they were ready to follow him anywhere.

THIS EXCHANGE MADE THIS WEDDING A PLACE OF GRACE.

(3) The law was exchanged for grace. This ceremony of washing hands—that's what these jars had been used for—was now replaced with something new.

(4) The Law of Moses was exchanged for a place of mercy. The exchange made this wedding a Place of Grace. We are cleansed by the blood of the cross. If you have to keep going back and completing this ceremonial washing of hands, you are constantly reminded that it is not enough. You just get unclean again. One more animal sacrifice. Again and again. Now we have been washed in the blood of the Lamb. We have moved. Now we live in a Place of Grace.

CHAPTER 2:

Saying Grace

"Jesus is saying that through God's grace, each of us has the strength to leave negative attitudes behind and be healed."

—MIKE NORMAN

Acts 27:27-35 (NASB)

"But when the fourteenth night came, as we were being driven about in the Adriatic Sea, about midnight the sailors began to surmise that they were approaching some land. They took soundings and found it to be twenty fathoms; and a little farther on they took another sounding and found it to be fifteen fathoms. Fearing that we might run aground somewhere on the rocks, they cast four anchors from the stern and wished for daybreak. But as the sailors were trying to escape from the ship and had let down the ship's boat into the sea, on the pretense of intending to lay out anchors from the bow. Paul said to the centurion and to the soldiers, 'Unless these men remain in the ship, you yourselves cannot be saved.' Then the soldiers cut away the ropes of the ship's boat and let it fall away. Until the day was about to dawn, Paul was encouraging them all to take some food, saying, 'Today is the fourteenth day that you have been constantly watching and going without eating, having taken nothing. Therefore I encourage you to take some food, for this is for your preservation, for not a hair from the head of any of you will perish.' Having said this, he took bread and gave thanks to God in the presence of all, and he broke it and began to eat.

As YOU GATHER AROUND THE TABLE EACH YEAR FOR YOUR Thanksgiving meal, you likely start by giving thanks—a time of prayer to thank God for all the blessings we enjoy. You might begin by saying, "Let's pray." Or, "Would someone like to say the blessing?" We sometimes call it "saying Grace." Ever wonder where this practice came from? Why do we do this? Matthew records two instances of Jesus feeding thousands of people—both times with only a small amount of food. In both cases, we see that Jesus broke the bread and then gave thanks to God for his provision.

In Acts 27, we read about the apostle Paul as he is sailing to Rome. Their lives were in great danger, so Paul took some bread and gave thanks to God. In the face of great danger, Paul stopped to pray and eat. On another occasion, actually on the day of the resurrection, Jesus was walking on the road to Emmaus and was joined by two of his followers. Once they arrived at Emmaus, Jesus stopped to eat with them.

The Scripture says Jesus then took the bread, gave thanks, and gave it to them. This seemed to be a regular practice for Jesus. Paul practiced this as well. The word grace comes from two Latin words—one means Grace and the other means thankful.

The answer is really quite simple as to why we do this. Our prayer is a reminder that everything we enjoy—although we work to buy the Thanksgiving food—we then go shopping and purchase all of it, and then spend an entire day getting it all ready. We must still remember, "Every good thing and every perfect gift is from above." [5] If it were not for Him, we would have nothing. Most of us don't find it difficult to be thankful when we sit down to a feast with plenty of food, plenty of conversation, and plenty of chocolate pie. What about when we are struggling?? What if it just hasn't been your year? What if you feel God has forgotten about you?

- Perhaps you have lost a loved one

- Now another family member is also seriously ill

- Bills are piling up and then your car breaks down

- Family members call you and none of them can make it to be with you

- Perhaps you're just not feeling very grateful

How do you say grace when everywhere you look, there are problems? In this passage we find the apostle Paul. The Bible says that for the fourteenth night in a row, his boat was being blown across the Adriatic Sea when suddenly all the men on board sensed they were approaching land. Becoming afraid that the boat would now crash against the rocks, they dropped anchor and prayed for daylight. Paul stopped right in his tracks, right where he was to do two things. (1) Stop and get some perspective. (2) Pray for daylight. He then dropped four anchors to hold them in place. Paul immediately expected that now was not the time to go any further. There is a time to sit still. The Bible says, "Be still and know that I am God."[6] There is also a time to get some perspective—o look around and determine where we go from here. Because right now things look pretty bleak. There is dangerous territory ahead. The writer here says they had already taken soundings. It tells us in verse twenty-eight. This is the only time we see this word in the entire New Testament. They took along some line or very thin rope and fastened pieces of lead to it. They would then drop it into the water until it hit rocks or the bottom. The line would be premeasured with pieces of leather at certain places telling them how deep they had gone. They measured and found that the water was one hundred twenty feet deep. They did it the second time and now it was ninety feet deep. They were in danger of being shipwrecked and that's when they dropped anchor. They stopped, and Paul began to pray.

What is the first thing you do when trouble is on the horizon? You know it is coming. You realize your life is about to be ship wrecked. You are about to crash. What do you do? Most of us do one of the following.

- We just go ahead and prepare for the crash. We give up. There is nothing we can do at this point, so we just sit back and wait for the crash.

- Often we go into worry mode. When I do crash—when everything falls apart—what is my life going to look like? When all of my dreams or all of my hopes are about to be dashed on the rocks, all I can do is worry. Glenn Turner says, "Worry is somewhat like a rocking chair: it gives you something to do but you don't get anywhere."[7]

- Others of us go into denial. We keep running at full steam, heading straight for a crash, hoping things will change. Denial is a defense mechanism. Many people with addictions use it, even their family members use it. They don't want to admit their family member has a problem.

Truth is, we all do it from time to time, and here is why. It takes care of the moment, but it does nothing to solve the problem. When life is about to crash, we really have one good option—stop and pray and look at our options. It's time to do something different because if you don't, you're going to crash. This is the time to stop and "say grace." Remember, Paul says be thankful in all circumstances—not **for** all circumstances, but **in** all circumstances. He said this because he knew that when we find ourselves in difficult circumstances, we need to stop and pray not—from a heart that is filled with worry, or a mind that is filled with denial, but from a heart is filled with gratitude.

It's never good to forget all the good God has done for your good. "Every good and perfect gift comes down from the Father" and we need to be reminded of that truth daily. Too many times we only focus on the crash that's ahead of us, or on all the bad that is around us. If there is anything that grace can offer us when we are facing difficult times, it is perspective. Grace has the ability to

ATTITUDE HAS BECOME A NEGATIVE WORD RATHER THAN A POSITIVE ONE.

completely change our outlook and to give us a completely new attitude. We are good at giving grace to others, but we are terrible about practicing it in our own lives. We can forgive others but we can't forgive ourselves. Attitude has become a negative word rather than a positive one. We might ask someone, "What is wrong with your attitude?" or say to them, "I think you need an attitude adjustment!" When we develop an attitude of gratitude, it makes all the difference in the world. Our attitude can affect our workplace, our family, and even the church. The remarkable thing is this, we have a choice to make every day. We cannot change our past, and we cannot change how other people act. Too many times we cannot change the crash that is about to happen right in front of us. We can change our outlook and our attitude. Chuck Swindoll said, "I am convinced that life is 10% what happens to me and 90% how I react to it."[8] Learn to focus daily on what really matters.

Rudyard Kipling was a great British poet whose writings have blessed many of us, including a generation gone by. Kipling was a very famous writer even before he died, and made a great deal of money at his trade. A newspaper reporter came up to him once and said, "Mr. Kipling, I just read that somebody calculated that the money you make from your writings amounts to over $100 a word." Mr. Kipling raised his eyebrows and said, "Really, I certainly wasn't aware of that." The reporter cynically reached into his pocket and pulled out a $100 bill and gave it to Kipling and said, "Here's a $100 bill Mr. Kipling. Now you give me one of your $100 words." Kipling looked at that $100 bill for a moment, took it, folded it up, and put it in his pocket and said, "Thanks."[9]

Pastor Jack Hinton had the opportunity of leading music for a worship service on the island of Tobago in a small leper colony. He said there was time for one more song, so he asked for a request from the congregation. A woman who had been facing away from the pulpit turned toward him and raised a hand that had no fingers. Her nose was entirely gone. Both of her ears were basically missing and most of her lips were gone. Her entire body was covered with sores from leprosy. Pastor Hinton said he could hardly bear to look at her, but he asked her "and what would you like for us to sing?" She asked, "Could we sing *Count Your Many Blessings*." The pastor said he was so overcome with emotion he had to leave the service. One of his church members followed him out the door and said, "Brother Jack, I guess you'll never be able to sing that song again." The pastor said, "Yes, I will, but I'll never sing it the same way again." [10]

CHAPTER 3:

The Power of Grace

*"Grace is the voice that calls us to change and then
gives us the power to pull it off."*

—MAX LUCADO

Romans 8:1-8 (NASB)

"Therefore there is now no condemnation for those who are in Christ Jesus. For the law of the Spirit of life in Christ Jesus has set you free from the law of sin and of death. For what the Law could not do, weak as it was through the flesh, God did: sending His own Son in the likeness of sinful flesh and as an offering for sin, He condemned sin in the flesh, so that the requirement of the Law might be fulfilled in us, who do not walk according to the flesh but according to the Spirit. For those who are according to the flesh set their minds on the things of the flesh, but those who are according to the Spirit, the things of the Spirit. For the mind set on the flesh is death, but the mind set on the Spirit is life and peace, because the mind set on the flesh is hostile toward God; for it does not subject itself to the law of God, for it is not even able to do so, and those who are in the flesh cannot please God.

ARTHUR DOYLE, WHO CREATED THE SHERLOCK HOLMES mysteries, loved to play practical jokes on his friends. His friends were of great character and very highly respected. Many of them were quite famous. For a joke, Doyle sent twelve of them the same identical telegram— "Leave at once, you have been found out." Within twenty-four hours all twelve men had taken a trip out of the country. [11]

No matter how great our reputation, we all have things of which we are ashamed and we hope no one finds out. The only solution for a guilty conscience is the forgiveness of Jesus Christ.

Let's talk about our failures. If you have never failed, never made a mistake, never committed a sin, then you're free to stop reading now. Since that is not the case for any of us, let's continue. At some point in life, we have all failed. Satan wants for us to never forget that. He wants us to dwell on our failures—from the moment we get up until we go to bed at night, and perhaps even dream about them all night. Guilt can bury us. What God wants is for us to learn something from them.

A farmer's favorite mule fell into a well. After studying the situation, the farmer came to the conclusion that he couldn't pull the mule out, so he might as well bury him. It was the humane thing to do. He got a truck load of dirt, backed up to the well, and dumped the dirt on top of the mule at the bottom of the well. When the dirt hit the mule, he started snorting and pounding his legs on the dirt, and as he did he began to get up on top of the dirt. Each time the dirt fell, he would just shake it off and step up. He did that until the dirt completely filled the well and then he just walked away—filthier, dirty, but much wiser. What was intended to bury him turned out to be his salvation.

When you and I get stuck in a deep well of dirt and sand and have to live with its consequences, there is not much that is worse. It's a terrible experience, so here's a truth to remember. Sin is the most destructive power known to man. We see in Verses 1-3, man was condemned. For me, part of the power and the beauty of Romans 8 is where it falls in Paul's letter. In the previous chapter, Paul took a look at his own life, evaluated it and said, "I do not understand what I do. For what I want to do I do not do, but what I hate I do. I know that nothing good lives in me, that is, in my sinful nature. For I have the desire to do what is good, but I cannot carry it out. What a wretched man I am! Who will rescue me from his this body of death?"[12] If Paul had ended his letter to the church in Rome right there, this would be one of the most depressing passages of Scripture in all the Bible. Luckily, he continues as we look in Verse 25 and he says thanks be to God— it's Jesus Christ our Lord! Thanks be to God. It is Jesus who rescues us! Bible scholars have argued concerning this passage for years debating this question—was Paul a believer at the time he wrote this, or was he speaking as an unbeliever?

For me, there are two basic arguments that clearly show that Paul was a believer at this time. First, an argument from experience. You would probably argue that there are times when you do things or say things and then wonder why you did them. You know the right thing to do, and you still don't do it. I can identify with Paul in this passage. Secondly, there is the argument from its placement in scripture. We believe Paul was saved in A.D. 34, died in A.D. 66, and likely wrote Romans in A.D. 56. Twenty plus years after he was saved, he wrote this. This passage in no way diminishes my opinion of Paul because I can completely identify with him, and if you're honest, you can too. There simply are times in all of our lives when we do not sense the power of his grace in our lives. Sin has a way of doing that to us. It is powerful and can destroy us.

God has broken the power of sin. God has set us free by sending his son Jesus Christ. However, this freedom we have does not mean we will never sin.

- David committed adultery and murder and God said, "You are a man after my heart."

- Peter denied Jesus three different times and Jesus said, "I will build my church on this kind of faith."

- Saul committed murder—killing Christians on many occasions. How did God respond? He called Paul into the ministry. That's is what grace is all about. It is grace at its best.

This should be a great relief to all of us for several reasons. First of all, even the saints who wrote Scripture, some who performed miracles—also struggled with the reality of sin. Next, it shows us that God has already done this difficult work for us. Satan sets a trap for God's people in hopes we will fall into it and many do. Paul said to Timothy, "It was his hope that we would come to our senses and escape the trap of the devil."[13] Satan sets the trap in hopes we will fall in. Here is the good news—when Jesus went to the cross, sin was defeated once and for all. What you and I need to understand is that because of grace, sin doesn't have the power to hold us prisoner. When Jesus went to the cross, he bore all of the sins of mankind—past, present and future. The weight of that sin was so heavy that Jesus cried out, "Why have you forsaken me?" The weight was so heavy at that moment, he felt completely alone. The late Dr. Billy Graham said that he believed that when Jesus was on the cross, he had you and me on his mind. As he hung there for six hours, he was calling out the names of all those who would experience His powerful grace. Through his grace, he has broken the power of sin.

We must learn to refuse the power of sin. In verses 5-8, Paul tells us something very important—the mindset our sinful nature desires is that sinful nature. The opposite can also be true. If we set our minds on what the spirit desires, we will live according to the spirit. One mindset leads to death, the other leads to life. Look at James 1:13-15, "When tempted, no one should say God is tempting me. For God cannot be tempted by evil, nor does he tempt anyone; but each one is tempted when, by his own evil desire, he is dragged away and enticed. Then, after desire has conceived, it gives birth to sin; and sin when it is full-grown, gives birth to death." These steps are progressive. If you could go back through the steps from death to sin, from sin to the birth of sin, from the birth of sin to the desire to sin, you come back to the point of our own evil desires. If at that point we can put on the mind of Christ when these desires try to take over, we can then refuse the power of sin. That is because of grace. It is that easy and it is that hard at the same time.

Paul tells us that if we really want to please God, this is what we must do. Paul reminds us, "I beseech you therefore, brethren, by the mercies of God, that ye present your bodies a living sacrifice, holy, acceptable unto God, which is your reasonable service. And be not conformed to this world: but be ye transformed by the renewing of your mind, that ye may prove what is that good and acceptable, and perfect, will of God."[14] In other words, we refuse to conform to the world. We exercise the power God has put inside of us and we choose to let the power of grace have its full effect on our lives. Let me share the testimony of two individuals. Ted Bundy, a serial killer told the press that his road to prison started with one look at a pornographic magazine.[15] Let that sink in. He said one look and he was immediately addicted. Max Lucado, said, "I came from a family of alcoholism and he said if there is anything to this DNA stuff; if it is genetic in other words; that I've got it." He chose not to drink, and it was never an issue until one day he said I lowered my guard a bit. He said "I was at a barbecue and I thought, hey, one beer won't hurt." Then he was having some Mexican food and he thought, hey, one more won't hurt.

BECAUSE OF GRACE, SIN CAN NO LONGER HOLD US AS A PRISONER.

Then he wasn't eating anything and he thought, hey, one or two more won't hurt. One day he was on his way to speak at a men's conference and he started thinking, where can I buy a beer and not be seen by anyone I know? So he drove by a convenience store, parked and waited until he would be the only customer in the store. He went in, got one, held it close to his side, and hurried to his car. He said right away he felt a sense of conviction and he remembered that just the night before he had had a long talk with his daughter about not covering things up. He chose to refuse. He got out, threw it in the trash, and asked for forgiveness.[16] We must learn to refuse the power of sin or it can destroy us. We must learn to live apart from sin. We must learn to be separate. Paul said, "If you live according to the flesh you are going to die."[17]

Not long after the Korean War, a Korean woman had an affair with an American soldier and became pregnant. He went back to the United States and she never saw him again. She gave birth to a little girl who looked different than the other children. In that culture at that time, that was unacceptable. Many women in that culture would in fact kill their children because they didn't want them to face rejection. She didn't do that. She tried to raise her little girl as best she could until the rejection became just too much. She did something that probably none of us could imagine ever doing. She abandoned her little girl to the streets.

This young girl was constantly ridiculed. They called her horrible names. It didn't take long for this little girl to draw conclusions about herself based on the way that people treated her. For two years she lived on the streets until finally she made her way to an orphanage. Then one day word came that a couple from America was going to adopt a little boy. All the children in the orphanage got excited because at least one little boy was going to have hope that day. This little girl spent the day helping the little boys get ready by cleaning them up, combing their hair, and wondering which one would be adopted by this American couple.

The next day the couple came in. This is what the little girl recalled. She said it was like Goliath had come back to life. "I saw this man with his huge hands lift up each and every baby. I knew he loved every one of them as if they were his own. I saw tears running down his face and I knew if they could, they would've taken the whole group of kids home with them." She said, "Then he saw me out of the corner of his eye. Let me tell you, I was nine years old but I weighed less than 30 pounds. I was a scrawny little thing. I had lice in my hair and boils all over me and scars all over my body. I was not a pretty sight." She said this man came over to her and he began saying something in English she couldn't understand and she looked up at him. Then he took his hands and laid them on her face. He was saying, "I want this one. This is the child for me."[18] With all of our scars and with all that is wrong with us and with all the terrible consequences our sin has put on us, grace is still available. God still wants us. God still wants you.

CHAPTER 4:

Face to Face with Grace

"Grace is the face that love wears when it meets imperfection."

—JOSEPH COOKE

John 11:1-3; 14-17 (NASB)

"In the beginning was the Word, and the Word was with God, and the Word was God. He was in the beginning with God. All things came into being through Him, and apart from Him nothing came into being that has come into being."[14] "And the Word became flesh, and Dwelt among us, and we saw His glory, glory as of the only begotten from the Father, full of grace and truth. John testified about Him and cried out, saying, 'This was He of whom I said, 'He who comes after me has a higher rank than I, for He existed before me.' For of His fullness we have all received, and grace upon grace. For the Law was given through Moses; grace and truth were realized through Jesus Christ."

THERE IS A PERIOD OF TIME BETWEEN THE CLOSING OF THE Old Testament and the beginning of the New Testament that lasted four hundred years. It is often referred to as four hundred years of silence because God's people did not receive any prophetic word during that time. No Scripture was written. As Paul says, "But when the fullness of time had come, God sent forth his son born of a woman subject to the law. God sent him to buy freedom for us who were slaves so that he could adopt us as his very own children."[19] Imagine. Four centuries of silence. No Scripture was written. No prophecy was given. However, some prophecies from the book of Daniel were fulfilled during that time. God was silent in speaking to his people. Have you ever felt that way? "Lord, where are you? Have you forgotten my telephone number? Have you forgotten where I live?" If it helps you at all, let me tell you, I have been there! It happens to all of us. Pastors are certainly not exempt.

Writers experience a condition commonly known as writers block. We want to write but we cannot seem to get started. It is how many writers make a living so it becomes very important. It happens to pastors. Pastors call it sermon block. Sundays come around with great frequency—every week—and pastors are thinking and praying early in the week, asking God to give us a fresh message for the week. There are times when we struggle and there are also times when we place our pen on the paper and can hardly write fast enough to keep up with what God is saying to us.

Let's face it. Most of us are not pastors. Most of us are not writers, but we still know what it's like to not have a fresh word from God. John tells us in Chapter 1, verse 1, "In the beginning was the Word and the Word was with God and the Word was God." "Word" is mentioned three times in that one verse and each time it is capitalized. It is the Greek word *logos* and this verse makes it clear that before there was a beginning the Word/logos was equal with God. Several thousand years later after the Old Testament was written, here in the gospel of John we learn that, "The Word became flesh and began to live among us." This gives us three principles that are extremely important in reading God's word.

(1) The Word is eternal and personal. Jesus is the Word.

(2) Jesus wants to have a personal relationship with his people.

(3) That relationship is only possible because of grace.

Every word we read in the book of John and every word we read in the New Testament must be read with these three statements in mind. Jesus is the Word. Jesus wants to have a personal relationship with his people. This relationship is possible because of grace. These three statements, and of course the entire gospel of John, are foundational to our faith. Cults will take Scriptures like John 1:1 and twist them to say things like, "In [the] beginning was the Word and the Word was with God and the word was a god." There are at least 2 phrases that have been twisted here.

(1) The addition of the letter a. A God. In other words, one of many.

(2) God is also not capitalized.

All of this was done to diminish the authority of Jesus by placing him as one of many gods and also diminish the authority of Scripture. Jehovah's Witnesses will not tell you who translated the New World Translation. They simply say it is anonymous. However, a relative to one of the men who has left the Jehovah's Witness faith has published a list and only one of them has actually studied the Greek language and that was limited. Not one of them has a solid background in the Greek language. Their interpretation is considered to be very biased and inaccurate.

Jesus is God. He is nothing more. He is nothing less. Anyone who teaches that He is less than God is not speaking the truth. This is what John is saying to us. If someone asked me, "Pastor, I want to read the Bible, but there are sixty-six books here. Where do I start?" My answer is to start with the gospel of John. If someone says, "Well, I have known the Lord for a long time and I want to go deeper in the Scripture. What should I be reading?" My answer is the same. Read the Gospel of John. The deepest you can go in Scripture is when you read the words of Jesus.

Now look at Verse 15. John testifies concerning Jesus. Look at it also in this translation. John testified about him when he shouted to the crowds, "This is the one I was talking about when I said, someone is coming after me who is far greater than I am, for he existed long before me." Now how does this work? Someone is arriving on the scene very soon. He is greater than I am and the reason is He existed long before me. It's slightly confusing, but it doesn't have to be. We can sum it up in just three words. **Jesus is eternal.** Before time began He was, He is now, and He always will be. He wants to have a personal relationship with you and me. Let's look at how that works. First if all it starts with grace.

Verse 14 tells us, "He is the one who came from the Father, full of grace and truth." Verse 16 says that from the fullness of his grace, we have been blessed. Verse 17 says that grace and truth came through Jesus Christ. It is grace that makes all of this possible. Without grace we would still be lost. Romans 8:3 tells us that, "The Law of Moses was unable to save us because of the weakness of our sinful nature. God did what the law could not do. He sent his own son in a body like the bodies we sinners have." We begin this relationship by praying for God's grace to fall on us. It is through grace that we are saved. It is through grace that our sins are forgiven. God forgives us and He forgets our sin. He will remember it no more.

We then begin a new life as we walk with Jesus daily. What does that look like? First and foremost, it is a walk of grace. Paul tells us in Colossians 1:6, "The same Good News that came to you is going out all over the world. It is bearing fruit everywhere by changing lives, just as it changed your lives from the day you first heard and understood the truth about God's wonderful grace." In chapter 2:6 he says, "so then just as you received Christ Jesus as Lord continue to live in him." In other words, in the same way you started, you must continue. Paul was speaking to church members who were strug-

WE START, CONTINUE, AND FINISH WITH GRACE. GRACE IS EVERYTHING.

gling with living by grace because they had previously been taught to live by the law. We often do the same thing. We just don't realize it. Living by the law is based on what we do. Living by grace is based on who we are and what we can be in Christ. This is why we are not called human doings. We are called human beings. Don't ever live with the lie that because you are not doing something, you are not valuable. Your value has nothing to do with your performance. It has everything to do with grace. We start with grace. We continue with grace. We finish with grace. Listen to what Paul said in the book of Acts 20:24 (NLT). "But my life is worth nothing to me unless I use it for finishing the work assigned me by the Lord Jesus-the work of telling others the good news about the wonderful grace of God."

Soren Kierkegaard, a great theologian from the nineteenth century, tells the story of a prince who was running an errand for his father one day in the local village. The prince passed through a very poor section of town. Looking through the window of his carriage, he saw a beautiful young peasant girl walking along the street. He could not get her off his heart. He continued to come to the town, day after day, just to see her and to feel as though he was near her. His heart longed for her, but there was a problem. How could he develop a relationship with her? He actually had the power to order her to marry him, but he wanted this girl to love him from the heart of her own free will. He could put on his royal garments and impress her with all of his servants, and drive up to her front door with soldiers and a carriage drawn by six horses. However, if he did this, he would never be sure that she loved him or was simply impressed with his power, his position, and his wealth. Instead, he came up with another idea. He gave up his kingly robe and all of his symbols of power and moved into the village dressed only as a peasant. He lived among the people, shared their interests, and talked their language. In time, the girl got to know him and fell in love with him.[20]

This is exactly what Jesus has done for us. The Word became flesh. The King of Heaven came down from His throne and put aside his heavenly robes. He came to us as one of us. He lived among us, ate with us, and drank with us, all to win us over. Could He have forced us? Absolutely! Instead, He chose to romance us. He invites us to come face to face with His amazing grace. He invites us to continue by grace and He encourages us to finish by grace.

CHAPTER 5:

Dealing with Blind Spots

"We all have a blind spot and it's shaped exactly like us."

—Junot Diaz

John 9 (NASB)

"As He passed by, He saw a man blind from birth. And
His disciples asked Him, 'Rabbi, who sinned, this man or
his parents, that he would be born blind?' Jesus answered,
'It was neither that this man sinned, nor his parents; but
it was so that the works of God might be displayed in him.
We must work the works of Him who sent Me as long as
it is day; night is coming when no one can work. While I
am in the world, I am the Light of the world.' When He
had said this, He spat on the ground, and made clay of
the spittle, and applied the clay to his eyes, and said to

him, 'Go, wash in the pool of Siloam (which is translated, Sent). So he went away and washed, and came back seeing. Therefore the neighbors, and those who previously saw him as a beggar, were saying, 'Is not this the one who used to sit and beg?' Others were saying, 'This is he, still others were saying, 'No, but he is like him.' He kept saying, 'I am the one.' So they were saying to him, 'How then were your eyes opened?' He answered, 'The man who is called Jesus made clay, and anointed my eyes, and said to me, 'Go to Siloam and wash'; so I went away and washed, and I received sight.' They said to him, 'Where is He?' He said, 'I do not know.' They brought to the Pharisees the man who was formerly blind. Now it was a Sabbath on the day when Jesus made the clay and opened his eyes. Then the Pharisees also were asking him again how he received his sight. And he said to them, 'He applied clay to my eyes, and I washed, and I see.' Therefore some of the Pharisees were saying, 'This man is not from God, because He does not keep the Sabbath.' But others were saying, 'How can a man who is a sinner perform such signs?' And there was a division among them. So they said to the blind man again, 'What do you say about Him, since He opened your eyes?' And he said, 'He is a prophet.' The Jews then did not believe it of him, that he had been blind and had received sight, until they called the parents of the very one who had received his sight, and questioned them, saying, 'Is this your son, who you say was born blind? Then how does he now see?' His parents answered them and said, 'We know that this is our son, and that he was born blind; but how he now sees, we do not know; or who opened his eyes, we do not know. Ask him; he is of age, he will speak for himself.' His parents said this because they were afraid of the Jews; for the Jews had already agreed that if anyone confessed Him to be Christ, he was to be put out of the synagogue. For this reason his parents said, 'He is of age; ask him.'

SO A SECOND TIME THEY CALLED THE MAN WHO HAD BEEN blind, and said to him, 'Give glory to God; we know that this man is a sinner.' He then answered, 'Whether He is a sinner, I do not know; one thing I do know, that though I was blind, now I see.' So they said to him, 'What did He do to you? How did He open your eyes?' He answered them, 'I told you already and you did not listen; why do you want to hear it again? You do not want to become His disciples too, do you?' They reviled him and said, 'You are His disciple, but we are disciples of Moses. We know that God has spoken to Moses, but as for this man, we do not know where He is from.' The man answered and said to them, 'Well, here is an amazing thing; that you do not know where He is from, and yet He opened my eyes. We know that God does not hear sinners; but if anyone is God-fearing and does His will, He hears him. Since the beginning of time it has never been heard that anyone opened the eyes of a person born blind. If this man were not from God, He could do nothing.' They answered him, 'You were born entirely in sins, and are you teaching us?' So they put him out. Jesus heard that they had put him out, and finding him, He said, "Do you believe in the Son of Man?" He answered, 'Who is He, Lord, that I may believe in Him?' Jesus said to him, 'You have both seen Him, and He is the one who is talking with you.' And he said, 'Lord, I believe.' And he worshiped Him. And Jesus said, 'For judgment I came into this world, so that those who do not see may see, and that those who see may become blind.' Those of the Pharisees who were with Him heard these things and said to Him, 'We are not blind too, are we?' Jesus said to them, 'If you were blind, you would have no sin; but since you say, 'We see,' your sin remains.

Yes it's a lengthy passage but to know the whole story we must read the whole story. The first sign Jesus performed was changing the water to wine. This is the sixth. Remember that a sign is a miracle that always points to a deeper truth and you will see that as we move through this passage. The disciples and Jesus were traveling together when they saw a man who was blind. Somehow they recognize that the man had been blind from birth. Immediately the disciples asked Jesus a theological question. "Teacher, who sinned, the blind man or his parents? Who caused this blindness?" One of the teachings from the Old Testament law came to be known as the Deuteronomic Formula which stated, if you do good, good things will happen, and if you do bad, bad things will happen. They would have known that teaching and they chose to follow it. This is likely why they asked the question. Jesus tells them quickly—neither of them sinned. There is in fact a bigger reason this has happened. God puts himself on display through his people so that the lost can be reached.

Remember, a sign always has a larger purpose than just the miracle in itself. The miracle mattered. If you don't believe it, ask the blind man. His world was completely changed. Jesus then goes to work immediately and he has an interesting formula to cure blindness. Dirt plus spit plus water equals new eyesight. The doctors at the local eye clinic may not support this procedure, but it worked for Jesus. Jesus basically made mud pies, then rubbed them on the man's eyes. He then instructed the man to go and wash in the Pool of Siloam. There was an underground tunnel that had been dug that extended about one third of a mile between the main spring and the pool, so the water could be circulated for use by the people.[21] The man went and washed the mud away and came back seeing. People recognized the man. He had probably sat in the same location daily, apparently to ask for money or food and his neighbors noticed him and said, "Hey, that's the guy we have seen begging." Some agreed. Others said, "No it's not him." The man says to them, "Yes I am the one!" Now they have a question for the man who had been blind. How did this happen? He explained the process. Dirt plus spit plus water equals new eyesight. These neighbors brought the man to the Pharisees. This group, the Pharisees, are mentioned dozens of times in Scripture. They loved the law and they were quite legalistic. Needless to say, none of this made any sense to them. They asked again. We want a different answer—one we understand—because this doesn't fit our theology. The man gives them the same answer and now they come to this conclusion. This man was blind. Jesus spread mud on his eyes. Now the man can see. This man, Jesus, does not honor the Sabbath. You see their thought was that anyone who kept the Sabbath rules could not heal, because that made them a sinner. If a man was a sinner, he could not perform miracles. Never mind that a man who was blind had been miraculously healed. Apparently this did take place on the Sabbath, and putting mud on his face involved work and that was not allowed to happen.

This demonstrates just how far they twisted the law to benefit themselves. What happened would occur many more times. The Pharisees and other unbelievers would miss the big picture. Jesus did not come to abolish the law. He came to fulfill it. In Matthew 5:17, Paul says the Old Testament law was our guardian and our protector until Christ came.[22] Then everything changed. Legalists don't like change—they don't know why they do things a certain way. It may not even be the right way or the best way. It is just what they had been taught.

You may have heard the old fable of the man whose wife sent him to the store to buy a whole ham. After he bought, it she asked him why he didn't have the butcher cut off the end of the ham. He asked his wife why she wanted the end cut off. She replied that her mother had always done it that way and that was reason enough for her. When the wife's mother was visiting and he ask her why she had always cut off the end of the ham. She said, "Well, it was because my pan was always too small to cook it in one piece." This describes the Pharisees for sure. Again, they asked the man who had been blind for an explanation for a third time. This is what he had to say about the one who healed him. He is a prophet. Now remember, John the Baptist was the first prophet these people had seen for over four hundred years, so this was a big deal. A prophet roaming around Israel, healing blind people? Impossible! The lawyer comes out in them and they say, "We don't like this witness, we want a new one." Let's talk now to the parents. Their first question to the parents is to clarify. Is this your son, the one you say was born blind? How then does he now see? The witness says, "Yep, that's him but we have no clue how he can see. Ask him yourself." I'm guessing at this point that the parents are experiencing a mixture of elation and fear—elation because he can see, and fear because they could be banned from the synagogue. We believe that Christians were already being persecuted for their faith. The beginning of that tradition of excommunication could've been right there in Jerusalem. Again they call the blind man to give glory for his healing to Jehovah God, not to Jesus, accusing Jesus of being a sinner. The blind man responds by just offering the simple truth. "Look guys. Whether he is a sinner or not, I don't know—in fact I don't care. This is the one thing I do know. I was blind and now I can see." Nothing else really matters. If you have experienced healing of any disease you know the feeling. Was it the chemotherapy, the radiation, or was it the surgery? Maybe it was just a good medical staff. Does it really matter? We just want to be well. That is what happened. What do they do? They asked him again. Their method of operation seems to be—if we just keep badgering the witness and if we keep asking the same question, perhaps we will get the answer that we want.

By this time the fellow is mildly aggravated. I can imagine his tone here as he says, "I already told you and you didn't listen. Why must I say it again?" Then he poses a question to them. Do you want to become his disciples too? They come right back and said, "Look, we follow Moses. We know God has spoken to him." They were likely thinking, "Remember, he's the one that went up on the mountain and got the Ten Commandments. He's the one that raised his staff and parted the Red Sea. This man (referring to Jesus), we don't know where he is from."

The blind man then says well that's amazing—you don't know where he is from but he gave me sight. Who cares where he's from! Again they fire back with their shortsighted theology and said God is not involved in this because God doesn't listen to sinners. We've never heard of anyone having their sight returned. Now you may not recognize that there is no history of this ever happening at this point. There's no Old Testament record of anyone being healed of blindness. None. When we examine the ministry of Jesus, there are more instances of the healing of the blind than any other miracle He performed. Seven to be exact.

They don't like his answers, so the Scripture says they threw the man out—probably meaning out of the synagogue. Early in my ministry I served a small country church—a farming community—and I read some of the history of the church while I was there. I found that they had thrown one young girl out of the church because she had gone on a hayride. Apparently the Pharisees are still with us today.

We pick back up at Verse 35. Jesus now stands up for the man they have thrown out of the synagogue. He asked the man a simple question. Do you believe? The man asks innocently, "Who is the Son of Man? Tell me so that I may believe." Jesus says, "I am He." The man then says, "I believe Lord" and he falls down and worships him.

Here is a principle I have learned from reading scores of books on the topic of leadership. Leaders must model the way, because people follow what they see. MindTools.com now says that sixty-five percent of learners are visual. Eighty-nine percent of what we learn, we learn visually.[23] That is why the apostle Paul would say, "Remember what you saw in me and then do it." The blind man saw for the first time, and he understood. He then believed. There are many things that can be blind spots for us— others see them—but we don't. It takes someone who does see them to point them out. All of us have them. If you have never given your life to Christ, I guarantee you there is a blind spot in your life. There's something that you have not been able to see as of yet that will allow you to make this particular choice to follow Christ. Today could be the day that you open your eyes for the first time to the gospel.

> **LEADERS MUST MODEL THE WAY BECAUSE PEOPLE FOLLOW WHAT THEY SEE.**

CHAPTER 6:

Not Guilty

"Guilt, according to scripture, is a condition; not a feeling."

—DAVID HENDERSON

Psalm 32 (NASB)

"How blessed is he whose transgression is forgiven, Whose sin is covered! How blessed is the man to whom the Lord does not impute iniquity, And in whose spirit there is no deceit! When I kept silent about my sin, my body wasted away Through my groaning all day long. For day and night Your hand was heavy upon me; My vitality was drained away as with the fever heat of summer. Selah. I acknowledged my sin to You, And my iniquity I did not hide; I said, 'I will confess my transgressions to the Lord;' And You forgave the guilt of my sin. Selah. Therefore, let everyone who is godly pray to You in a time when You may be found; Surely in a flood of great waters they will not reach him. You are my hiding place; You preserve me from trouble; You surround me with songs of deliverance. Selah. I will instruct you and teach you in the way which you should go; I will counsel you with My eye upon you. Do not be as the horse or as the mule which have no understanding, Whose trappings include bit and bridle to hold them in check, Otherwise they will not come near to you. Many are the sorrows of the wicked, But he who trusts in the Lord, lovingkindness shall surround him. Be glad in the Lord and rejoice, you righteous ones; And shout for joy, all you who are upright in heart.

I HAVE NOTICED IN THE LAST YEAR OR SO THAT ON CERTAIN menus in restaurants and on certain items in the grocery store that they now offer certain food items that are "guilt free." This also may mean they are taste free.   I mean let's face it, sugar tastes good. Apparently there are people who when they eat certain things they feel guilty. I am not one of those people. Maybe you are. However, brings up a couple of thoughts about this thing called guilt. First, there are some people who suffer from an overactive conscience. They feel guilty about things when they shouldn't. Have you ever noticed that some people beat themselves up over these things. For others, it doesn't bother them. I remember one of the teenagers in our church telling me, "Pastor, I ate a whole package of chocolate cookies." To this, I responded, "Wow you're my hero." As a result, he didn't feel an ounce of guilt over it. Some of us would beat ourselves up for a week if we did that.

That brings me to the second thing I want to say about guilt. Guilt can be self-inflicted. Not all guilt comes from God. There can be times when you or I have committed a sin and we feel guilty, so we pray and ask for forgiveness and we still feel guilty. Psalm 32 was written by the Psalmist David. David was a good man. The Bible describes him as a "man after God's own heart." As good as David was, he was far from perfect and he knew what it felt like to feel guilty. David was a shepherd boy who was chosen one day to become the King of Israel. The Bible tells us that after he became king, there came a day when his troops were out to war and David decided to stay home. Homes in that era often had a ladder of sorts attached to the house and you could climb

IN SCRIPTURE, GUILT IS A CONDITION, NOT A FEELING.

up on top and sit and look at the stars, etc. One evening, David was there and he noticed a beautiful woman named Bathsheba who was bathing. David found her to be attractive so he called for her to come to his palace. Both David and Bathsheba were already married, just not to each other. An affair takes place. Not long after that, Bathsheba informs David that she is pregnant with his child. David knows he is guilty, so now he figures he needs to come up with a plan as to what to do. He calls Bathsheba's husband, Uriah, in from the battle field to spend the weekend with his wife. His hope is that they will have relations that weekend and then when the baby is born, Uriah will think it is his. What he didn't consider was that Uriah, being a very faithful man, both to his wife and to the King, said, "I cannot go to my wife this weekend because I will not seek pleasure while my fellow soldiers are all out fighting." As a result, David still had a problem—a faithful soldier and a pregnant woman. He decided to have Uriah killed. King David sends Uriah up to the front lines of battle by telling the captain of the army that Uriah is a traitor and he wants to put him up in the heat of battle and then pull all the other troops back. That is exactly what happened and Uriah was killed in battle. Now his problem is solved, David thought. You would think that everything was solved now. There was still one problem. Guilt.

The Bible shows us there is a distinct difference in being guilty and in feeling guilty. They are not the same thing. David is guilty. He has committed adultery and then committed murder. A year passes and then what was seemingly a secret sin now is an open scandal. God sends Nathan the prophet to speak to King David. Nathan confronts him and says, "Look, God knows what you have done." David, now being confronted with his guilt, falls to his face and cries out, "I have sinned!" When you read Psalm 51, you almost feel like you are walking into David's private prayer room because this prayer is very personal and very private as we hear him cry out, "Wash me clean from my guilt. Purify me from my sin. For I recognize my shameful deeds; they haunt me day and night."(Psalm 51:2-3 NLT)

We can see clearly that the reason for David's guilt is simple. Sin. David committed several sins that had an effect on his relationship with Bathsheba, her husband Uriah, his soldiers, and ultimately with God. Of course it affected him. Read his words again in Verses 3 and 4. He is weak. He is hurting. He is drained. Why? Because he was silent. He didn't try to cover it up, didn't rationalize it, didn't try to hide it, or ignore it. He simply confessed it. The word "confess" in the Bible means to agree with. He agreed with God. He came clean. Chuck Swindoll said, "Secret sin and inner peace cannot coexist."[24] David had no peace. It was affecting him physically, emotionally, and spiritually. His strength was gone. He was sorry—not just sorry that he got caught—he was genuinely sorry. David prayed for forgiveness and God gave it.

There is more. There is our adversary, Satan. He has a part in your guilt. His name means "accuser," so that is exactly what he does. He accuses. His desire is to paralyze you with his guilt. By achieving this, your witness will no longer be effective. He whispers to you, "Hey what you did...there's no forgiveness for that ...you've gone too far." Don't play his game. Read this carefully. There is no sin that is beyond the reach of God's forgiveness. None. There is also our part. Confession. 1st John 1:9 says, "If we confess our sin, he is faithful and just to forgive our sins and to cleanse us from all unrighteousness." Confession is the key. Revealing is the beginning of healing. There are some of you who have carried your sin around for a lifetime. I have one word for you. Stop. Stop carrying it around.

There is also God's part. Forgiveness. He will forgive and He will forget. We have to remember that just because we can't seem to forget, that doesn't change the fact that God CAN and DOES. He will remove them as far as the east is from the west. Think about that. I'm glad He doesn't say as far as the North is from the South. Have you ever heard of an east pole? We have North, South but not an East pole or a West pole. You can start going East and you can stay going east forever. David is mentioned fifty-seven times in the New Testament. He is an Old Testament figure, but still very well known in the New Testament. Fifty-seven times, but NEVER once is his sin mentioned. You know why? Because it is gone! Yours can be as well. You can move to a place of grace.

CHAPTER 7:

Love Letters in the Sand

"Every heart sings a song, incomplete, until a heart whispers back.
Those who wish to sing, Always find a song."

—PLATO

John 7:53-8:11 (NASB)

"Everyone went to his home. But Jesus went to the Mount of Olives. Early in the morning He came again into the temple, and all the people were coming to Him; and He sat down and began to teach them. The scribes and the Pharisees brought a woman caught in adultery, and having set her in the center of the court, they said to Him, "Teacher, this woman has been caught in adultery, in the very act. Now in the Law Moses commanded us to stone such women; what then do You say?" They were saying this, testing Him, so that they might have grounds for accusing Him. But Jesus stooped down and with His finger wrote on the ground. But when they persisted in asking Him, He straightened up, and said to them, "He who is without sin among you, let him be the first to throw a stone at her." Again He stooped down and wrote on the ground. When they heard it, they began to go out one by one, beginning with the older ones, and He was left alone, and the woman, where she was, in the center of the court. Straightening up, Jesus said to her, "Woman, where are they? Did no one condemn you?" She said, "No one, Lord." And Jesus said, "I do not condemn you, either. Go. From now on sin no more."

THE WORD GRACE HAS NOW BEEN IN USE FOR SEVERAL thousand years. It is one of those words we still use today that comes right out of the Scripture and most of us use it as though we understand exactly what it means. Just a few examples:

- Our insurance company gives us a *grace period*.

- We say someone has *fallen from grace*.

- Musicians have what is called a *grace note*. Some play it. Some don't. It's optional.

- When a dancer performs, we might say she is graceful.

- We bow our heads and say Grace.

"Grace" is used in many ways. For me it is one of those words we cannot completely understand until we see it in action. Grace is something we must encounter in order to fully understand. I think most of us have settled for a definition of grace that is cheap and one that is less than what the Scripture actually intends. In this passage, the Pharisees were attempting to discredit Jesus. This is the dilemma into which they placed themselves. This woman had broken the Law of Moses. Just to refresh our memory this is what the law stated. "If a man commits adultery with another man's wife, he must be put to death." If Jesus chose to pardon this woman, it would show a lack of respect for the Law of Moses. It would mean that He took the Law of Moses lightly. On the flipside, if he agreed to put her to death, he would break Roman law under which the Jews were living. This is why John tells us in this passage in Verse 6, "They were using this as a trap, in order to have a basis for accusing him." In other words, they weren't really concerned about how this would affect the woman caught in adultery. Instead, they were really after Jesus. This should not surprise us.

- When Jesus had finished teaching in the previous chapter, John 7, the Bible says someone attempted to seize him.

- When Jesus healed the man on the Sabbath, the response of the Pharisees was that they went out and conspired against him as to how they might destroy him.

- When the Passover was just two days away, we read that the chief priests and their teachers of the law were scheming to arrest Jesus and secretly kill him.

In fact, it seemed that with every action Jesus took to demonstrate his grace, this was their response. Jesus was saying, "I have a gift for you. It is free, it will set you free, and there is nothing you have to do to except receive it." Their response was, "We will destroy you!" It's strange how people often respond to God's grace.

Grace was never intended to be a problem; it was meant to be a solution. All of us know that man has had a problem from the beginning of time. Man was born with a propensity to sin. Our nature was bent in that direction. As a result, all of us have made some very bad choices in our lifetime. We have hurt people. In fact, many times we have hurt the people we love the most. We've spoken words we wish we could reel back in, and we've done things that when we look back on those actions, we look in disbelief that we would do that. It is a terrible problem—one that we do not know how to deal with, and we were left with no one to turn to. Then, along came Jesus. Before anyone else, Jesus recognized that you and I have a problem with sin. The woman caught in adultery faced a problem that looked unsolvable. The deck appeared to be stacked against her.

The teaching of the Old Testament was clear. Adultery was a crime punishable by death. It is now illegal in at least fourteen countries including Afghanistan, Nigeria, Pakistan and others. In ten countries of the world, homosexuality is also punishable by death.[25] This woman who had been caught in the act knew exactly what she was facing. You cannot help but quickly notice that she was brought in by the teachers of the law. This group shared one thing in common—they were all men. The man who was caught in the act was apparently released. At least they knew something about grace, but it was a selective grace—a cheap grace, a grace of convenience.

Grace is not a convenience for a few. It is a gift for all. The Bible is clear in Romans 3:23. His grace is for anyone who believes. Male, female, white, black, young, old, married, or single. It is a gift. To prove this point, this is what Jesus does. He bent down and started to write on the ground with his finger. The same finger many of us use to ridicule someone, to point at and say, "You are guilty." It is the same way we point at someone to cast shame on them, but Jesus used his finger to erase all of her sin and shame and guilt. What did he write? We don't know. John doesn't tell us. Have you ever written a message in the sand? You probably did as a child if you grew up near a beach. Our oldest son, David Jr, in 2001, took his then girlfriend to a nice restaurant on the beach and at the right moment he excused himself from the meal for five to ten minutes, then came back to the table. She had no idea what he was doing. He took her by the hand for a brief walk on the beach, and there in large letters in the sand he had written, "Will you marry me?" She said "yes," by the way. It was a love letter written in the sand. Some have speculated that Jesus was writing down the sins of everyone who stood there. Others say he was writing down Scripture from the Old Testament. The truth is we do not know.

Whatever he was writing, it was the greatest love story ever told. It was an act of grace, an act of forgiveness for a woman who was no doubt very afraid, completely broken, and heavy laden with guilt. No doubt she felt unloved and ridiculed. In one short sentence, Jesus changed everything in her life. Like a governor issuing a pardon, he put his signature in the sand. I have to believe that whatever Jesus wrote in the sand was connected to the next words he spoke. "If any of you is without sin let him be the first to throw a stone at her." It was the perfect reply. It had nothing to do with the law. It had everything to do with grace. Then he does an interesting thing. He wasn't finished. He stooped down and wrote on the ground again. Everyone there had time to think about their own lives and conviction had no doubt set in.

Grace must be experienced. It can be life-changing if we will just receive it. I have had individuals on different occasions say to me, "Man, pastor I think you were talking directly to me today." I just figure the Holy Spirit is working on them. In this case, Jesus was trying to get a message out to the entire crowd—the Pharisees, the woman who was caught, and all the others who were bystanders. You wonder, "Why didn't anyone respond?" Jesus just gave an invitation there and they walked out, one by one. You see, they were really just there to do their job. Deuteronomy 17 says, "The witnesses of a crime who had reported it to the authorities would be the first to cast the stones." They were all too glad to do so. We love to point out the faults of others. Be honest. Some of us love it a little too much. We make light of other people's shortcomings and maybe even make jokes. Bullying has become rampant among young people, but it is nothing new. The reason people do it is because they

GRACE IS A GIFT.

STOP TRYING TO EARN IT.

YOU CAN'T.

don't feel so good about themselves, so they put someone else down in hopes they will feel better, at least for a moment. I love what happens here. Look at Verse 9. Do you ever wonder why did the older ones leave first? Were they more mature and they figured it out quicker? Did they suddenly recognize that their own sin was even greater and that this man named Jesus knew it? Again, the Bible doesn't tell us. We assume they drop their stones right then. They slipped away one by one until only

Jesus was left in the middle of the crowd with the woman. When I read this passage again, I think, "What crowd? Who is this crowd that remained?" Then I remembered in Verse 2 they are the ones who gathered to hear him teach. They didn't come for a stoning. They had heard of this man named Jesus and just wanted to hear what he had to say, but it all got interrupted. Instead of hearing it, they got to experience it firsthand, and that's what makes a difference. Jesus stood one final time and He asked the woman, "Where are your accusers?" She may have been cowering in the sand, afraid someone was going to throw a stone, so she likely looked around to realize she was all alone with Jesus.

That is when grace started for her. When did it start for you? Romans 8:1 tells us, "There is therefore no condemnation to those who belong to God in Christ Jesus." Romans 8:33-34 says, "Who can accuse the people God has chosen? No one, because God is the One who makes them right. Who can say God's people are guilty? No one, because Christ Jesus died, but He was also raised from the dead and now he is on God's right side appealing to God for us." This occurred for you and for me—to bring us to a place of grace.

CHAPTER 8:

Running from God

"Running from God is the longest race of all."

—THEODORE ROETHKE

Jonah 1:1-3 (NASB)

> The word of the LORD came to Jonah the son of Amittai saying, "Arise, go to Nineveh the great city and cry against it, for their wickedness has come up before Me." But Jonah rose up to flee to Tarshish from the presence of the LORD. So he went down to Joppa, found a ship which was going to Tarshish, paid the fare and went down into it to go with them to Tarshish from the presence of the LORD.

I READ A STORY RECENTLY OF A FIVE-YEAR-OLD BOY WHO decided to run away from home. The woman who lived next door saw him leave as she was cutting her grass. She watched him as he walked up and down the sidewalk in front of her house, dragging his little suitcase behind him. He would then disappear around the corner and a few minutes later he would reappear and go past her again. After he had gone past her house several times, she finally asked him, "What are you doing?" He said, "I'm running away from home." She says, "Well, why do you keep circling the block?" He says, "Because my mom and dad won't let me cross the street by myself."

Let me ask you. Have you ever wanted to run away from home— just leave everything and go someplace where no one can find you? At one time or another, I would say that every one of us has felt like that. There was a problem or a situation or a person that we just wanted to get away from, and the only solution seemed to be to run. Psychologists use a term to describe this called the "flight or fight" syndrome. It is said that when we are placed in a very difficult situation, it is usually our tendency to do one of two things—fight the problem and try to solve it, or run away. Jonah chose to run away. In fact, there is a long history in the Bible of men and women running away from God. In Genesis after Adam and Eve sinned, the Bible says that they ran away and hid from his presence. We looked at Moses after he killed a man. He ran away. David ran away from King Saul and hid in a cave. When Jesus was arrested in the garden, the disciples ran away. Now we come to Jonah. When we studied the Book of Jonah in seminary, our OT professor told us there were three ways this book can be interpreted. He concluded by saying that he believed it was a literal story—it happened just as the scripture says. He quoted Billy Graham who said, "If the bible says that Jonah swallowed the whale, I would still believe it." I agree.

I heard a story once about a little girl in elementary school who was in class one day studying about the ocean when the teacher told the class, "I don't want any of you to ever be afraid of going into the ocean because there are no sea creatures that can swallow you whole.

This little girl raised her hand and said I learned in church that a great fish swallowed Jonah whole. The teacher just wrote it off and said, "That's impossible. That could never happen." The little girl said, "When I get to Heaven, I'll ask Jonah myself and find out if it was true." The teacher replied, "Well what if Jonah didn't go to heaven?" The girl then said, "Then maybe you can ask him."

The facts are that only three verses in Jonah deal with the big fish. The other forty-five verses tell the story of Jonah. Again, there are three ways we can view this story.

1. It can be symbolic. The characters and the events you read have a deeper meaning. They are telling a story, but the events did not actually happen.

2. It can be seen as a parable. Some believe it is a parable describing the deliverance of Israel.

3. It is historically accurate and based on real events. This is what I believe and always have. The primary reason I believe that the story happened exactly this way is because Jesus accepted it as such.[26]

When the scribes and the Pharisees asked Jesus for a sign to prove that what He said was true, He said, "An evil and adulterous generation seeks after a sign and no sign will be given to it except the sign of the prophet Jonah. For as Jonah was 3 days and 3 nights in the belly of the great fish so will the Son of Man be 3 days and 3 nights in the heart of the earth." The other thing I want to point out before we dive into Chapter One is that neither the Old nor New Testament call the fish a whale. It is simply called a great fish.

Early in the book of Jonah we find these truths.

1. God still invites us to join Him in His work.

2. The call comes to Jonah to go in this direction to preach to the people in Ninevah, but instead Jonah runs away and goes in the opposite direction. We don't know how God spoke. He spoke audibly to Adam and to Abraham. He spoke in a vision to Ezekiel. He spoke in a dream to Joseph. We don't know how, we just know that He did speak. He has many ways of speaking to us—through a sermon, through His word, or through a song. God still speaks to His people.

3. When He speaks, we may not like what He says. There are times when God gives us an assignment that is difficult. When God gives us an assignment, it is always something we cannot do without Him.

Ninevah was a rising, powerful city in the day of Jonah. It was also home to Jonah's enemies, so it was the last place Jonah thought God would ever send him to preach. You see, Ninevah was just not a very nice place. They did a lot of evil things. The Bible tells us in Chapter Four

RUNNING FROM GOD MEANS ONE SIMPLE THING. YOU ARE GOING IN THE WRONG DIRECTION.

that Jonah was very angry that God was sending him there. Let me ask you, have you ever been given a job to do that you really didn't want to do? I'm sure you have. I have. God told Jonah to go down to Ninevah and preach, but Jonah didn't like these people. They were mean and Jonah didn't think they deserved salvation. Instead, he decided to run and that's when his trouble started. Jonah was not in this boat by himself.

Has something ever happened to someone you didn't like very much? Perhaps they hurt you and then you heard about their misfortune, and instead of feeling sorry for them you threw a party. Ever felt that way? If you have, please don't write and tell me. If God has ever asked you to go to someone and ask forgiveness, to go and apologize, to go to share Christ with someone, but you refused, then you are just like Jonah. Jonah was looking for the easy way out. When God speaks, we may not like what He says.

4. Running from God means one simple thing. You are going in the wrong direction. Verse. 3 tells us that Ninevah is to the east. Tarshish is to the west. God has given us this wonderful thing called free will. We are not puppets. We can do as we please and if we choose to run away from God, we can. That doesn't mean He won't come after us. He does this because He knows that the only place we will find peace is in the middle of God's will.

CHAPTER 9:

Lost and Found

"When my soul was in the lost and found—you came to claim it."

—CAROLE KING

Luke 15:11-32 (NASB)

"And He said, 'A man had two sons. The younger of them said to his father, 'Father, give me the share of the estate that falls to me.' So he divided his wealth between them. And not many days later, the younger son gathered everything together and went on a journey into a distant country, and there he squandered his estate with loose living. Now when he had spent everything, a severe famine occurred in that country, and he began to be impoverished. So he went and hired himself out to one of the citizens of that country, and he sent him into his fields to feed swine. And he would have gladly filled his stomach with the pods that the swine were eating, and no one was giving anything to him. But when he came to his senses, he said, 'How many of my father's hired men have more than enough bread, but I am dying here with hunger! I will get up and go to my father, and will say to him, 'Father, I have sinned against heaven, and in your sight; I am no longer worthy to be called your son; make me as one of your hired men.' So he got up and came to his father. But while he was still a long way off, his father saw him and felt compassion for him, and ran and embraced him and kissed him. And the son said to him, 'Father, I have sinned against heaven and in your sight; I am no longer worthy to be called your son.' But the father said to his slaves, 'Quickly bring out the best robe and put it on him, and put a ring on his hand and sandals on his feet; and bring the fattened calf, kill it, and let us eat and celebrate; for this son of mine was dead and has come to life again; he was lost and has been found.' And they began to celebrate. "Now his older son was in the field, and when he came and approached the house, he heard music and dancing. And he summoned one of the servants and began inquiring what these things could be. And he said to him, 'Your brother has come, and your father has killed the fattened calf because and his father came out and began pleading with him. But he answered and said to his father, 'Look! For so many years I have been serving you and I have never neglected a command of yours; and yet you have never given me a young goat, so that I might celebrate with my friends; but when this son of yours came, who has devoured your wealth with prostitutes, you killed the fattened calf for him.' And he said to him, 'Son, you have always been with me, and all that is mine is yours. But we had to celebrate and rejoice, for this brother of yours was dead and has begun to live, and was lost and has been found.'"

THE FIRST TWO WORDS OF THIS PASSAGE YOU JUST READ ARE, "Jesus continued." We should go back for a moment and see exactly what Jesus was talking about. We find very quickly that Jesus is actually sharing three separate stories—three separate parables all giving us the same lesson. The first is the parable of the lost sheep. The Bible tells us that the tax collectors and sinners had gathered to hear him teach and one of them said this man welcomes sinners and let's eats with them. This was grace at its finest. Jesus hung out with the bad guys. He clearly came to offer grace to those who were sick.

The story is simple. A man has one hundred sheep and loses one of them. How do you do that? I am told it is not that difficult. Sheep like to wander. It is a problem shepherds have experienced for thousands of years now. They are in the pasture eating, and they eat with their heads down, buried in the grass, and they don't know when to stop eating. They walk and walk until they are no longer a part of the group and when they finally look up, they are lost and have no clue where they are. The Shepherd must go out and find him. He goes to a great deal of trouble to find him and then bring him home. In the second para- ble, a woman has ten silver coins and loses one of them. She basically turns everything upside down looking for it. When she finds the coin, she calls all of her friends and neighbors together to tell them. Then we come to the third story we know as the parable of the prodigal son. The father has two sons, the younger one leaves home, the father grieves over him leaving, and the son goes out and falls into the wrong crowd.

All three of these parables share several things in common:

1. Something is lost. A lamb, a coin, a son.

2. That item is extremely valuable. There is nothing more valuable to a shepherd than one of his lambs. This was his livelihood. This is how he fed his family. They were an investment for him and every one of them mattered. So he leaves other ninety-nine sheep to go and find the one.

3. In each case, the owner has the same goal—to bring the lost item home.

In the second parable, a woman has ten silver coins and she loses one of them. Each of these coins was a drachma and was worth about a day's wage. There was nothing perhaps more valuable to a woman in the day of Jesus than her money. Most women had very little. In the third story, we see there is a lost son. The father had two sons. It is the younger of the two who comes to him and basically says, "Hey, Dad, I want my inheritance." We have no indication here of why he wanted it, nor do we understand why the father gave it to him so quickly. Apparently he wanted to be on his own. If you have raised children, or you are raising them now, at some point you will hear them say, "I can't wait until I can live on my own. I don't like it here. I'll be glad when nobody tells me what to do and I can do whatever I want to." When that day arrives, most young people realize it's not as easy as it sounds. This young man distanced himself as far as possible from his family. He also took up a new lifestyle. He probably said to himself, "Now I can do whatever I want, buy the things I want, go to work if I feel like it, or stay

home if I feel like it. No one is the boss of me." He apparently didn't
have much experience in how to handle money, and he realized that he
had more month that he has dollars. Then a famine came and he had
no food and no work. It was not a good place to be. However, this man
was fortunate. He found a job. He was a Jew and he was hired to feed
pigs in a pigpen. For the Jews living by the law of the Old Testament,
the Scripture was clear. Leviticus reminds us that the pig was considered unclean. "You shall not eat of their flesh nor touch their carcass"
This was a part of their dietary laws which were written to help them
stay healthy. Most of us eat pork today. Pork chops, ribs, sausage, pork
roast, and how about bacon? Now the good news is we don't live under
this Old Testament law, but pork is not exactly health food. Bacon may
be a whole food group for you. Grains, vegetables, bacon—I think chocolate is one too, right? Here is a Jew who cannot eat pork. He cannot
even touch the pig if the pig dies, yet his job is feeding pigs in a pigpen.
In the end, he fattened the pigs and starved himself. The Bible says he
was so hungry he wanted to eat the pods—the shell of bean/pea. Like
two peas in a pod. It was not real food. It was used as slop for the hogs.
If you've ever been near a pigpen, there is one thing you know—you
don't want to eat out of there. Remember the kid named Pigpen in the
Charlie Brown comics? The images were not good, and this is where
he worked. He chose to starve himself. Notice in Verse 17, he comes to
his senses. He recognizes, "Hey, I don't have to live in this pigpen.' He
says the people who work for my father have plenty of food. They have
food to spare, and here I am starving to death." After realizing this, he
decides to go back home. Here is his plan. He will say three things: (1)
Father I have sinned, (2) Father I am not worthy to be called your son,
and (3) Make me like one of your hired servants. Then he got up and
went to his father. This is where grace enters the story. In case you didn't
catch it, the son didn't call his dad, didn't send him a text, didn't put

his picture on Facebook. He doesn't say, "Here I am in the pigpen dad. I'm coming home." There was zero communication between the son and his father, but we learn some important truths here.

1. Grace waits on the doorstep for you and me. We don't know how long the son had been gone, but we get the distinct feeling that he stood there for days waiting. That's what grace does. Grace waits. Grace is patient.

2. Grace is always willing to take the first step, if necessary. As soon as the father spots his son, he leaps off the front porch and runs to him, throws his arms around him, and kisses him.

3. Parents often recognize things their children don't see. This young man was going off with his share of the inheritance, venturing out for the first time in his life to make it on his own! The problem is he wasn't ready and somehow the father knew it. How do I know that? Because he was standing there waiting for him. Did your parents ever do that? Wait up for you? This father waited perhaps for days, even weeks. When he sees his son, he runs out to meet him. The family feud is over. His son is home and nothing else matters.

GRACE IS ALWAYS WAITING ON THE DOORSTEP FOR YOU AND FOR ME.

4. Grace makes repentance much easier. The son has already rehearsed what he plans to say. Remember, "Father I have sinned. Father, I'm not worthy. Make me one of your

servants." Look at Verse 2. He never gets to the last one before grace speaks up. It's as though the father doesn't even hear what his son has to say. Grace has a way of accepting apologies very quickly. You don't have to beg grace for forgiveness. You don't have to make promises. You don't have to bargain with grace, "I'll do this if you'll do that." Grace is free.

Grace is more than we deserve. Grace is better than we can imagine. It can't be bought. It can be earned. It's free. Why do we miss this? Some of us cannot get beyond the idea that we have to do something in order to get it. Jesus loves you, this I know, for the Bible tells me so.

CHAPTER 10:

Get out of Jail Free

"I would rather a thousand times be a free soul in jail than to be a sycophant and coward in the streets."

—EUGENE U. DEBS

Matthew 6:1-18 (NASB)

"Beware of practicing your righteousness before men to be noticed by them; otherwise you have no reward with your Father who is in heaven. So when you give to the poor, do not sound a trumpet before you, as the hypocrites do in the synagogues and in the streets, so that they may be honored by men. Truly I say to you, they have their reward in full. But when you give to the poor, do not let your left hand know what your right hand is doing, so that your giving will be in secret; and your Father who sees what is done in secret will reward you. When you pray, you are not to be like the hypocrites; for they love to stand and pray in the synagogues and on the street corners so that they may be seen by men. Truly I say to you, they have their reward in full. But you, when you pray, go into your inner room, close your door and pray to your Father who is in secret, and your Father who sees what is done in secret will reward you. And when you are praying, do not use meaningless repetition as the Gentiles do, for they suppose that they will be heard for their many words. So do not be like them; for your Father knows what you need before you ask Him. Pray, then, in this way: 'Our Father who is in heaven, Hallowed be Your name. Your kingdom come. Your will be done, On earth as it is in heaven. Give us this day our daily bread. And forgive us our debts, as we also have forgiven our debtors. And do not lead us into temptation, but deliver us from evil. For Yours is the kingdom and the power and the glory forever. Amen. For if you forgive others for their transgressions, your heavenly Father will also forgive you. But if you do not forgive others, then your Father will not forgive your transgressions. Whenever you fast, do not put on a gloomy face as the hypocrites do, for they neglect their appearance so that they will be noticed by men when they are fasting. Truly I say to you, they have their reward in full. But you, when you fast, anoint your head and wash your face so that your fasting will not be noticed by men, but by your Father who is in secret; and your Father who sees what is done in secret will reward you."

MEDICAL SCIENCE HAS BEEN TELLING US NOW FOR YEARS that there is a very close relationship between physical illness and stress. That shouldn't be hard for us to believe. When we go through a time of extended stress and difficulty, many times we become physically sick. I learned this week in fact that it is possible that up to eighty percent of those who are currently hospitalized, have a stress related illness. Eighty percent! Hospital chaplains have noticed also that many times there is a strong connection between the physical and spiritual. Jesus obviously knew this and we see this teaching being applied in the Gospel of Matthew in Chapter 9. A man who was paralyzed is brought to Jesus on a mat. Jesus heals the man and the Bible says that the man jumped up and went home. Amazing. If you read the passage too quickly, you will miss the words Jesus spoke to bring healing to the man. Jesus said, "Be encouraged my child, your sins are forgiven." Interesting words to speak to heal someone. Yet the words, "Your sins are forgiven" are possibly the most powerful words we can speak to someone who has hurt us, offended us, or damaged us in any way. Jesus teaches on this topic of forgiveness on numerous occasions and the results are always powerful. In Matthew Chapter 6, he addresses the topic again and it is here that He tells us how to pray and He concludes with a powerful statement about forgiveness. We need to look at all of these verses to fully understand what Jesus was saying. There are actually at least four topics he addresses here—giving, praying, forgiving, and fasting. He addresses them in that order. I want to look at each one briefly, but want to focus on the topic of forgiveness, because these topics have a definite connection.

When you give, give with the right attitude. It would be easy for me as a pastor to simply say, "I don't really care how you give, just as long as you give," but that's not what the Bible teaches. When you give, you must give with the right attitude. Here is the principle. When you give, give privately, not publicly. Jesus is letting us know right off the bat that if we give for the purpose of being seen by others, to impress someone, or to make some kind of righteous appearance, you will have no reward in heaven. This word reward runs through this passage like a red thread shows up on white material. In other words, it is very obvious. Seven times we will see it. It is a definite theme, and it is the theme that seems to connect these passages. I don't think most of us expect a reward when we give, but Jesus makes it clear that if we give with the right attitude, there will be one. Notice two things he tells us specifically not to do when we give—don't give for public applause, and don't tell others about your giving. Give in private.

In Jesus' day, there were large metal containers, like a box, right at the entrance to the temple that were used to collect monetary gifts. The box had a type of funnel at the top, larger at the opening than at the bottom. It was made of metal. If you were skilled and knew how to toss that coin in just the right way, it would ring out very loudly, like a trumpet. Never give for the applause or approval of others. "Then," He says, "don't tell others." Give privately. Don't let others know how much you are giving. Give in secret. Only then will you be rewarded.

Learn how to pray. Jesus gives us two principles here to follow. First, close the door and pray in private. Jesus wasn't saying not to pray in public. Jesus prayed publicly many times in front of others. He was simply saying to direct your prayers to the Father, not to impress others. Apparently there was a problem in that day with individuals standing out in public to pray to draw attention to themselves. Some would even stand on the street corner to get attention. Second, don't use a lot of words. After all, God will not be impressed with your vocabulary. He uses the phrase here, "Don't babble." If you recall the story of the Tower of Babel where the people decided to build a tower to stretch to the heavens, God intervened and caused them to speak in a variety of languages, stopping them from understanding one another, so they had to stop the project. Babylon was given its name for this reason. Today we still understand that babbling on and on, and using lots of words to impress, may impress yourself, but not others.

Now let's move to the topic of fasting and then we will come back to the topic of forgiveness. Beginning at Verse 16, he tells us in essence how to fast. He gives us some guidelines. Again there are two. First, when you fast, don't be so unhappy about it. He says don't be sad faced. Don't make your face unattractive to draw attention to yourself. I remember my roommate in college had done something to make his girlfriend upset and he was looking for a way to get out of it so he decided to do something to make her feel sorry for him so she would forget about what he had done. He took a pencil and a piece of paper, rubbed the lead off on the paper then rubbed it under his eyes, making him look really distressed. I told him he was nuts, but it worked. Jesus says don't make yourself look all sad. Instead be happy when you fast. Smile. Second, don't show your fasting to others, show it to the Father. Then and only then will you be rewarded.

This brings us to the topic of forgiveness. God will forgive us in same way we forgive others. If you don't think that's true, read Verses 14-15 again. In three of the four passages, the word "reward" comes up repeatedly.

- Verse 4. Give in secret, not to be seen. Then you will be rewarded.

- Verse 6. Pray in secret, not to be heard. Then you will be rewarded.

- Verse 18. Fast in secret. Then you will be rewarded. In other words, don't tell anyone and you will be rewarded. But here's the twist. Forgiveness often needs to be public. If you hurt someone in front of other people, you need to apologize to everyone. The more public the offense, the more public your apology should be.

Let's pull all of this together. There are three things here I want us to take note of. Jesus gives us first of all a prayer for forgiveness. The Bible describes what we call the unpardonable sin. Unforgivable. It is mentioned in two passages in the Bible, Mark 3 and Matthew 12. Basically, this is when our sin is unforgivable. It is when we refuse to accept the only remedy there is for sin, which is Jesus. It is when we are so far away from God that we do not even desire forgiveness. In other words if you

IF YOU HURT SOMEONE IN FRONT OF OTHER PEOPLE, YOU NEED TO APOLOGIZE TO EVERYONE.

refuse Jesus, you will not be forgiven. Everything else outside of that, no matter what sin you have committed, can be forgiven. In forty-five years of ministry, I have spoken to many people who believe they have done something that is so terrible they cannot be forgiven. Let me assure you that if you are afraid that you have committed that sin, you haven't. The person who has committed that sin doesn't care. They have completely turned irreversibly against Jesus.

In the model prayer, we read these words in Verse 12. "Forgive us our debts as we have also forgiven our debtors." We are to pray, "Lord forgive us in the same way we forgive others." Throughout history, men and women have prayed this prayer and have been forgiven. It is amazing that it is that simple. For some reason, we want to complicate forgiveness. We have convinced others that is not simple. It is difficult and there are hoops we must jump through. In other words, we are convinced somehow that we must earn it.

Here is the last thing about forgiveness. The best thing about forgiveness is that it is absolutely free. If you are trying to earn it, you're wasting your time. You cannot. There is a promise of forgiveness in Verse 14. According to Bible Gateway, there are five thousand four hundred sixty-seven promises in Scripture. This is one of them. If you forgive others, God will forgive you. God is the ultimate promise keeper. Forgiveness is a done deal if we ask. It is a promise God will never break. There is also a warning here for each of us. If you do not forgive others for their sin against you, God will not forgive you for your sin. Our immediate response to that statement might be, "Hey, that's not fair." It reminds me of a verse in first John that says, "Whoever claims to love God yet hates his brother is a liar." In other words, I do love God but Lord you don't understand. This other guy, this other woman, apparently you don't know them. They are nothing like you. To that, He essentially says, "I am going to treat you like you treat others. If you love me, you must love others as well. If you don't forgive others, I will forgive you." That's the message and perhaps one of the most important principles in Scripture. We really need to grasp this concept of forgiveness and practice it. If there is anything we need to understand, it would be forgiveness—how to get it and how to give it to others.

Harry Houdini, the famous escape artist, issued a challenge wherever he went. He could be locked in any jail cell in the country, he claimed, and set himself free quickly and easily. He always kept his promise, but one time something went wrong. Houdini entered the jail in his street clothes. The heavy, metal doors clanged shut behind him. He took a concealed piece of metal that was strong and flexible from his belt. He set to work immediately, but something seemed to be unusual about this lock. He worked for thirty minutes, but got nowhere. An hour passed, and still he had not opened the door. By now he was bathed in sweat and panting in exasperation, but he still could not pick the lock. Finally, after laboring for two hours, Houdini collapsed in frustration and fell against the door he could not unlock. When he fell against the door, it swung open! It had never been locked at all! In his mind it was locked and that was all it took to keep him from opening the door and walking out of the jail cell.[27] Forgiveness can be the same way. It can lock us up.

When there is bitterness, jealousy, or anger between you and another person, and you choose not to forgive, it can place you in jail. Not them. YOU. Choosing not to forgive keeps us from actually being forgiven. You know the peace that comes with forgiveness, and you know what it feels like when you don't have it. Peace comes from God and without forgiveness, we are empty, bitter, angry, and often even sick. Forgiveness is the remedy and we must go to Dr. Jesus to get it. You can set the prisoner free today because the prisoner is you.

CHAPTER 11:

Moving to the front of the Line

"When we are no longer able to change a situation, we are challenged to change ourselves."

—VICTOR FRANKL

Luke 8:40-55 (NASB)

"And as Jesus returned, the people welcomed Him, for they had all been waiting for Him. And there came a man named Jairus, and he was an official of the synagogue; and he fell at Jesus' feet, and began to implore Him to come to his house; for he had an only daughter, about twelve years old, and she was dying. But as He went, the crowds were pressing against Him. And a woman who had a hemorrhage for twelve years, and could not be healed by anyone, came up behind Him and touched the fringe of His cloak, and immediately her hemorrhage stopped. And Jesus said, 'Who is the one who touched Me?' And while they were all denying it, Peter said, 'Master, the people are crowding and pressing in on You.' But Jesus said, 'Someone did touch Me, for I was aware that power had gone out of Me.' When the woman saw that she had not escaped notice, she came trembling and fell down before Him, and declared in the presence of all the people the reason why she had touched Him, and how she had been immediately healed. And He said to her, 'Daughter, your faith has made you well; go in peace.' While He was still speaking, someone came from the house of the synagogue official, saying, 'Your daughter has died; do not trouble the Teacher anymore.' But when Jesus heard this, He answered him, 'Do not be afraid any longer; only believe, and she will be made well.' When He came to the house, He did not allow anyone to enter with Him, except Peter and John and James, and the girl's father and mother. Now they were all weeping and lamenting for her; but He said, 'Stop weeping, for she has not died, but is asleep.' And they began laughing at Him, knowing that she had died. He, however, took her by the hand and called, saying, 'Child, arise!' And her spirit returned, and she got up immediately....."

DURING THE THREE-AND-A-HALF YEARS JESUS SPENT IN PUBLIC ministry, there was an extended period of time when he enjoyed a great deal of popularity. On many occasions, Jesus would be completely spent from the demands that had been placed on him, so he would separate himself from the crowds to do as the Scripture says, "to come apart" to a solitary place. However, it was always like, "nice try, Jesus," because the crowds would always find Him. In fact, on one occasion, Jesus crossed the river to be alone and when he got there, they were waiting for Him. That is exactly what was happening in this passage, also. Everywhere that Jesus went, the crowd was sure to go. Therefore, it is not a surprise in this passage of Scripture when we see such a large group surrounding him. In a matter of moments, two individuals—one dying, the other suffering from what seemed to be an incurable disease, both came to him to be healed. JB Phillips explains in his book titled, *Your God is Too Small* that as a result of our upbringing, we can sometimes develop an inadequate perception of God. In other words, our God is too small.[28] In his book, he lists seventeen different images we seem to have created. For instance, God in a box. This is when we think we have captured God and placed him in a neat little box with labels all over it as though we know everything about him. The problem of course is that God thinks outside the box. He is very original. He spoke through a burning bush. He spoke through a donkey, but he only did each one time. Another is an image of God as an operator sitting at a switchboard trying to keep up with every request that comes in, but never has enough time to handle all of them. That is the theology many of us have developed. God is busy, everyone is trying to get to him, everyone has a need, and some of the needs are more important and some of the people are more important. After all, if my Pastor or the Pope is praying, surely He puts their requests ahead of mine. This must have been what this woman was thinking. Jairus, a leader in the local church, comes to Jesus, falls at his feet, and pleads for the life of his only daughter who is twelve and dying. She is a child, so this must be at the top of his list. It is like he proclaimed, "Clear my agenda and hold my calls. This matters."

As Jesus begins to walk with the man, he is surrounded by the crowd which includes a woman who had been suffering with constant bleeding, with no cure to be found for twelve long years. It is interesting that the girl who is sick is also twelve. This woman has bled for as long as Jairus' daughter has been alive. She apparently has no one to speak for her and she demands no attention from Jesus. There may think there are several reasons for this:

1. Her need is not as great.

2. She's not worthy because she's a woman.

3. She's not worthy because she is unclean.

She is simply not sure if she matters to Jesus. Thus, she thinks, "Maybe if I can just touch the fringe of his robe, the hem of his garment, then I won't be in the way of the more important things Jesus has to do." She was just waiting there for Jesus. Think about it. It was almost as though her hand was reaching out in praise and then she got a chance. She was close enough and she reached down and grabbed her opportunity—she stole a miracle. She took it without even asking. The Bible says that when she touched his robe, immediately the bleeding stopped. It's interesting that this word, "immediately" (the Greek word is eutheos) occurs eighty-one times in the Gospels. Apparently, Jesus never struggled with procrastination. He did things immediately.

He never struggled with multitasking either. Two people need healing, so on his way to heal one, he heals another. And he did it immediately. In other examples:

1. In Matthew, when he met a leper, the Bible says that as soon as he spoke the man was healed.

2. Again in Matthew, two men said, "Jesus we want to see." Jesus touched their eyes and instantly they could see.

3. In Mark, a man who was deaf and also had a speech impediment was brought to Jesus and Jesus touched him and said, "Be opened!" Instantly the man could hear perfectly and could speak plainly.

4. In John, there was a man at a pool who had been paralyzed for thirty-eight years. He laid by the pool every day, but couldn't get in. He said, "Someone else always gets ahead of me." Jesus said to him, "Pick up your mat and walk." The Bible says the man was instantly healed.

THERE IS NO ONE ON EARTH GOD LOVES MORE THAN YOU.

Why is it we think any of these things? "I'm not as important as they are." "God has bigger things to take care of than me." After all, world hunger, cancer, terrorism—the big stuff— haven't been taken care of yet. Let me tell you three things that really matter:

1. There is no one on Earth God loves more than you.

2. If you were the only person on Earth, He still would have gone to the cross for just you.

3. He invites you to move up to the front of the line to a place of grace.

CHAPTER 12:

Grace and Godliness

"Look for Christ and you will find Him.
And with Him, everything else."

—C.S. Lewis

Ephesians 4:7-17 NCV

"Christ gave each one of us the special gift of grace, showing how generous he is. That is why it says in the Scriptures, 'When he went up to the heights, he led a parade of captives, and he gave gifts to people.' (Psalm 68:18) When it says, 'He went up,' what does it mean? It means that he first came down to the earth. So Jesus came down, and he is the same One who went up above all the heaven. Christ did that to fill everything with his presence. And Christ gave gifts to people—he made some to be apostles, some to be prophets, some to go and tell the Good News, and some to have the work of caring for and teaching God's people. Christ gave those gifts to prepare God's holy people for the work of serving, to make the body of Christ stronger. This work must continue until we are all joined together in the same faith and in the same knowledge of the Son of God. We must become like a mature person, growing until we become like Christ and have his perfection. Then we will no longer be babies. We will not be tossed about like a ship that the waves carry one way and then another. We will not be influenced by every new teaching we hear from people who are trying to fool us. They make plans and try any kind of trick to fool people into following the wrong path. No! Speaking the truth with love, we will grow up in every way into Christ, who is the head. The whole body depends on Christ, and all the parts of the body are joined and held together. Each part does its own work to make the whole body grow and be strong with love."

THERE ARE 4 TRUTHS ALL OF US SHOULD KNOW.

1. Your identity and purpose are unique, like your fingerprints. There is no one exactly like you.

2. You and I were spiritual orphans, but God has adopted us into His family.

3. As a result, we have been justified—forgiven. Romans tells us, "There is now no condemnation for all who belong to Jesus." No condemnation. None.

4. God is not finished with us yet. Paul tells us, "I am sure of this, that he who began a good work in you will bring it to completion."

Now that we know these truths, we have a much better grasp of three other facts. We understand just how much God loves us—the height, depth, length, and width of God's love. We begin to understand our purpose, and we know our identity in Christ. There may be a question lingering for you. Now that I understand who I am in Christ and now that I have a better understanding of what He wants me to do, where do I find the strength and resources to do it? Where do I find this Place of Grace God has assigned to me? How will I find the strength to work through His assignment for my life? The answer is wrapped up in our Grace Gifts. Let's begin by defining that term to get a better understanding of what Paul means here.

The term, "Grace Gift" comes from the Greek word *charismata* which means, "unmerited favor." It is not deserved. It means something that is very good is being given to someone who is very undeserving. Paul also tells us in 1st Corinthians 12:4 that there are diversities of gifts. There are diversities of ministries. They are given for all. Everyone will profit from your individual gifts. They are given because all of us act like immature infants at times. For some it is even a lifestyle. We are not acting like spiritual grown-ups. We are still drinking milk, and Paul wants us to move to meat. That is God's desire, and it should be ours as well. After all, I would much rather have a big ribeye than a small glass of milk. Infants are cute when they are just born. They make us laugh. Once they grow older, it's no longer funny if they act like infants. It is cute when a baby:

1. Crawls around when they are about six months old, but not so much when they turn seven or eight years of age.

2. Suck their thumb at two to three months, but not so cute if they are six or seven years old.

3. Talk like a baby at age two, but there is something wrong if they do it at seven or eight years old.

It works the same way spiritually. It's just not as cute when someone has known Jesus for years but is still a babe in Christ. It is no longer acceptable if their walk and talk has not changed. It brings me to this thought. If spiritual change and growth are not taking place in our daily life, it is possible we have not actually experienced the second birth.

SALVATION IS MUCH MORE THAN FIRE INSURANCE OR A "GET OUT OF HELL FREE" CARD.

Please let that sink in. When you were saved, you were saved for two reasons, to provide you with an eternal home in Heaven, and to help you grow into the likeness of Jesus Christ. To be clear, you were saved for both reasons, but salvation is much more than fire insurance or a "Get out of Hell Free" card. Salvation gives us a new birth—everything changes. When we lead someone to Christ, we need to make sure this is not just about gaining a home in Heaven, praying the sinner's prayer, and then sitting back and doing nothing. This is about life change—complete life change. A new beginning. A second birth.

If you have not established your home in Heaven, I encourage you to do that today. Then, the moment you have, then move to spiritual growth. This involves giving of yourself in ministry, which brings us back to our earlier question. Now that I understand what I have in Christ and a better understanding of what Jesus expects from me, where do I find the necessary strength and resources? Our strength comes from the Holy Spirit who lives inside us. The resources come from the charismata—our Grace Gifts. They are developed through the preaching and teaching of the evangelists and the pastor—all who are teachers according to Paul. The foundation has been laid by the apostles and prophets. With that completed, the evangelists and pastor-teachers are used to build the super-structure the church requires to grow. It is not the task of these individuals/leaders to do all the work of the ministry. It is actually our task to prepare the people for service. When believers are equipped and accept their ministry, then the entire body is:

- Built up

- Mature

- Strengthened

- Flourishing

All of these diverse gifts, the charismata—these grace gifts—are for one purpose. They bring unity to the body. In God's eyes, there are no superstar pastors, none of us whose faith and knowledge are superior. His goal is twofold—to bring unity to the church and maturity to every believer. This will result in some amazing changes in the church.

- Believers will no longer act like children.

- Believers will no longer be persuaded to jump from one opinion or belief to the next.

- Believers will no longer listen to or follow false teaching.

- Believers WILL learn to speak the truth in love.

I believe that speaking the truth in love is a sign or mark of maturity. Immature believers often fall into one of two traps. They speak the truth in love, but do so without love, or they love without speaking the truth. When we do the former, we often hurt people. We pound them with the truth but there's no gentleness or love. When we do the latter, we don't tell others the truth, thinking that by shielding them from the truth that we are sparing then from pain. In actuality, we are not. All we are doing is delaying their ability to grow and mature. Every Pastor and every member must recognize that we all belong to one another. We need each other—no matter how insignificant you might think someone's contribution is. As Francis Schaeffer used to say, "There are not little people in the kingdom of God and there are no little jobs."[29]

As was the case with most of the churches to whom Paul wrote, the church in Ephesus faced false teachers with opposing viewpoints. This of course resulted in a division in the churches. If there is no unity, people act like infants—crying out because of their own needs—and all are at the mercy of deceitful teachers. Maturity involves teaching the truth in love. False teachers don't show love and don't care for the members. They only want one thing—their own way. It takes the entire body to work together in unity. Think about it. How can we work in unity if the whole body is not involved? In all of this we must remember it is God who is the head of the church!! No one else. The heavenly Father, as the head of the church, allows each part of the body to mature and grow. Every part, not a chosen few. Why? Because it takes all of us. It only takes one person to break unity in the Body. It is only because Jesus is the Head of the church that we can do anything that lasts. If we try to run the church in our own strength, it will surely fail. However, if we look to the Head of the church, Jesus Christ, nothing, I repeat, nothing is impossible. The body must be ONE and we must present ourselves as ONE, not divided as the world might see us. When churches fight within the church or with another church, we do irreparable harm to the cause of Jesus Christ. When the world begins to see us as ONE and we truly function as ONE, the world will change dramatically and the Kingdom of God will be ushered in. On Earth as it is in Heaven.

Have you ever seen a sequoia tree? They are found in abundance in California. They can grow to be thirty feet wide and two hundred fifty feet in height. It is amazing, but it is a fact. I spoke to an arborist who was taking a large oak tree out of our yard and he told me it was about thirty feet high, so the roots would be about the same length. That's how it is supported. That is not the case with the sequoia tree. Many of these trees are over three thousand years old, and are two hundred fifty feet in height but have roots that are barely below the surface of the ground.

Now you would think that a strong wind would blow one over, but here's the key. Even though the roots only go maybe twelve feet deep, the roots grow in groves. Groups of roots intertwine underground. When the strong winds come along, they hold one another up.[30]

That is a picture of how the church functions. We have to get together in groups. Our roots might be shallow, maybe just below the surface. If we stand alone, life will blow us over like a cheap umbrella. We have to wrap ourselves together in groups, and form a lifeline. By working together, we bring glory to the Father. By doing so, if the strong winds are going take any of us, they will take ALL of us. As long as there are enough of us, that's just not going to happen. We will stand together and grow together toward the SON, Jesus Christ.[31]

CHAPTER 13:

Grace under Fire

"Don't treat people as bad as they are, treat them as good as you are."

Luke 6:6-11 (NASB)

"On another Sabbath He entered the synagogue and was teaching; and there was a man there whose right hand was withered. The scribes and the Pharisees were watching Him closely to see if He healed on the Sabbath, so that they might find reason to accuse Him. But He knew what they were thinking, and He said to the man with the withered hand, "Get up and come forward!" And he got up and came forward. And Jesus said to them, "I ask you, is it lawful to do good or to do harm on the Sabbath, to save a life or to destroy it?" After looking around at them all, He said to him, "Stretch out your hand!" And he did so; and his hand was restored. But they themselves were filled with rage, and discussed together what they might do to Jesus."

WHEN WE'RE FACING A DIFFICULT TIME IN OUR LIVES, WE often describe life as being like a pressure cooker. Now for some who may not know, this is how a pressure cooker works. A pressure cooker is simply a pot that is sealed. It has a valve that controls the steam pressure inside. As the pot heats up, the liquid inside forms steam and that raises the pressure in the pot. The temperature then rises above the boiling point. As a result, the food cooks faster. This is great for cooking a meal, especially if you are in a bit of a time crunch, but it is a terrible place to live. When we live there and we are under constant pressure, all kinds of things can begin to happen. Our physical health will begin to deteriorate. We are tired all the time. Seventy-five percent to ninety percent of all doctor's office visits are for stress-related ailments and complaints. Forty-three percent of all adults suffer adverse health effects from stress.[32] In addition, our emotional health is affected. We begin to worry. All of our thoughts are based on a single question—when will this ever stop and how can I ever get out from under all of this pressure?

When our physical and emotional health are affected, we also see all of this taking an even greater toll on our spiritual lives to the point that we can no longer focus on the only one who can get us out. These cookers are fortunately designed with a valve and all you have to do is open the valve and when you do, it lets off steam and the pressure begins to go down. Don't you wish it were that simple to blow off your personal steam?

In this passage, we find Jesus in a pressure cooker of sorts. The Bible tells us that it was the Sabbath, so he went to the synagogue. He was chosen as the visiting teacher for the day. The focus quickly shifts to a man in the crowd whose hand was deformed/shriveled. The Pharisees were the power brokers of the day, and they spotted the man with this deformity. The crowd watched Jesus closely. Like laser vision, they honed in on Jesus, hoping to catch him in the act—of all things—helping someone. They tried to catch him in the act of doing something good. Parents catch their children with their hands in the cookie jar. Police with radar, hiding behind a bush, catch people speeding. These are both instances of being caught in the act of doing the wrong thing. Jesus was doing something good, but in their eyes he was breaking the law. This was the Sabbath. There were rules stating they could not do work of any kind on the Sabbath. For them, this included healing. If he did in fact heal this man, they planned to accuse him of working on the Sabbath. In the Old Testament, a man was found picking up sticks on the Sabbath. Moses told the people to take him out and stone him to death. That is what the law in the Old Testament stated should happen. The stakes were very high in this situation. On the flip side, Jesus had stated that he had come to heal the sick, not the healthy. If he chose to follow the law, instead he would be giving up his mission/purpose in life.

At this point, Jesus stepped into the pressure cooker. Have you been there? Two people pulling at you. One wants this, the other one, that. You are pushed into a corner. It is not going to be a win/win situation. It is a win/lose no matter what you choose to do. Verse eight tells us that Jesus had a distinct advantage here. Do you see it? "But Jesus knew their thoughts." You and I are not mind readers. We are not psychic, so we don't always know what someone else is thinking, but Jesus did. He could see right through to their hearts. We at times step from the frying pan to the fire and we only make matters worse. It becomes very difficult to make a good decision. I'm not talking about the simple everyday decisions we make. I'm talking about those that are extremely difficult because they have such a huge impact on our lives. A woman discovers she is pregnant, and the guy just walked out. She thinks, "What do I do?" Tough decisions. A man at work is told to look the other way when his boss is unethical in his business practices. If he doesn't, he could lose his job. A pastor is told if he doesn't buy a home through a realtor who attends his church, they will cause trouble for him. This actually happened to me. What about a man who is Muslim and becomes a believer in Jesus, but if he goes public his family will never speak to him again and he could even be killed? These are real events. And life puts us in a pressure cooker. Let's face it. Life is more difficult when the heat is on, and it becomes even more difficult to do the right thing. The very things I have been describing that we face, Jesus faced them as well, only on a deeper level. His life was actually hanging in the balance, depending on what decision he made. Most every time that Jesus was placed in a situation like this, it also became a teaching moment. He wanted them to recognize the purpose of the Lord's Day. At this point there was nothing but awkward silence.

Remember when Jesus spoke to those who brought the woman before him who had been caught in adultery? He got nothing but silence. The only sound you might have heard was the sound of the rocks they held dropping to the ground.   This time, Jesus speaks to the sick man and says to him, "Come and stand in front of everyone." In other words, "Let's just get this out in the open where everyone can see what I am about to do." No secrets here. Nothing hidden. Jesus then poses a question to his critics—the ones who have placed him in this position. We see it in Verse 9. "Then Jesus said to his critics, 'I have a question for you. Does the law permit good deeds on the Sabbath or is it a day for doing evil? Is this a day to save life or to destroy it?'"

What does this passage say to us? Let me share five things we can learn from this passage.

1. The Sabbath was made for us, not the other way around. Granted there are some things we don't need to do on Sundays. For the most part, we can shop on other days, buy gas on other days, and many of us don't have to work on Sundays. By the way, I do. If I don't show up on Sundays, there are consequences for me. No one wants a pastor who isn't willing to work on Sundays. If you have ever had to go to the emergency room on a Sunday, you are thankful for hospital staff who are there. When I worked at other jobs

THE SABBATH WAS MADE FOR US, NOT THE OTHER WAY AROUND.

while in college and seminary, I told them up front that I preferred not to work on Sundays, but was willing to work longer hours during the week. They always honored that. Never hesitate from doing good on the Sabbath simply because it is the Sabbath. Remember, Jesus is Lord of everything, including the Sabbath.

2. A day of rest and worship must be a priority for all of us. Too many times we are simply greedy and want to make more. This principle of rest was given to man because God knew that many of us would work twenty-four/seven—non-stop. Like many of you, I have gone through extended periods of time where I had no time off. I had to

learn the hard way that I am a better person when I take a regular day off. If you haven't noticed, the word recreation can also be pronounced re-creation.

3. You will never lead anyone into the kingdom by using the law. It is always about Grace. We are saved by grace. PERIOD. For at least 3500 years, Rabbis have given us all kinds of rules to go by. They include rules for farming, cooking, and sewing. You could make one stitch if necessary, but not two. If you raised sheep you could not do business on the Sabbath. If you raise cattle, you could not kill them for food on the Sabbath. You could not write more than one letter. You could not erase more than once. You could not build a fire, and if you had one left over from the previous day, you could not put it out. You could not turn electricity on or off. If it is on, you can't turn it off. If it is off, you can't turn it on. You will never lead anyone into the kingdom through legalism, but you will lead many into the kingdom through grace.

4. If you have an issue in your family, in your marriage, in your church, or between you and another friend, bring it to the forefront and talk about it. You may lose a job, but you should never lose a God-given conviction. There are many decisions in life that are tough, and they usually share one thing in common. If our beliefs are going to be compromised, if we will no longer be popular with other people, or if we are being threatened, then it gets tough. An old saying says, "When the going gets tough, the tough get going, but too often they just 'get going' right out the door." In other words, they run. You and I

share something in common today. We have a tendency to run from the tough decisions in life. We run from hard decisions.

One decision most of us have never had to make is this—what if we were to claim Christ as our Savior and then all our friends unfriended us for life. What if they wanted nothing to do with us? What if our family did the same? What if, as a result of your commitment to Christ, your family suddenly said, "You know what? You're dead to me!" I believe that as we go forward as a nation in the world as it is today that things are only going to become more difficult. We know just a few generations ago, we had prayer in school. We recited the Lord's Prayer. Now football coaches cannot lead in prayer on the field. Terrorism is rampant. Society is changing every day. More and more we have to worry about whether what we do or say is politically correct. It is time for our nation to turn back to our roots. "If my people who are called by my name will humble themselves and pray and turn from their wicked ways, then will I hear from heaven and will forgive their sins and will heal their land."[33] What we need more than anything is to get to a place of grace.

CHAPTER 14:

Breaking the Chains

*"I will break the chains behind me, happiness will find me.
Leave the past behind me, today my life begins."*

—YAO

Mark 5:1-20 (NASB)

"They came to the other side of the sea, into the country of the Gerasenes. When He got out of the boat, immediately a man from the tombs with an unclean spirit met Him, and he had his dwelling among the tombs. And no one was able to bind him anymore, even with a chain; because he had often been bound with shackles and chains, and the chains had been torn apart by him and the shackles broken in pieces, and no one was strong enough to subdue him. Constantly, night and day, he was screaming among the tombs and in the mountains, and gashing himself with stones. Seeing Jesus from a distance, he ran up and bowed down before Him; and shouting with a loud voice, he said, 'What business do we have with each other, Jesus, Son of the Most High God? I implore You by God, do not torment me!' For He had been saying to him, 'Come out of the man, you unclean spirit!' And He was asking him, 'What is your name?' And he said to Him, 'My name is Legion; for we are many.' And he began to implore Him earnestly not to send them out of the country. Now there was a large herd of swine feeding nearby on the mountain. The demons implored Him, saying, 'Send us into the swine so that we may enter them.' Jesus gave them permission. And coming out, the unclean spirits entered the swine; and the herd rushed down the steep bank into the sea, about two thousand of them; and they were drowned in the sea. Their herdsmen ran away and reported it in the city and in the country. And the people came to see what it was that had happened. They came to Jesus and observed the man who had been demon-possessed sitting down, clothed and in his right mind, the very man who had had the 'legion;' and they became frightened. Those who had seen it described to them how it had happened to the demon-possessed man, and all about the swine. And they began to implore Him to leave their region. As He was getting into the boat, the man who had been demon-possessed was imploring Him that he might accompany Him. And He did not let him, but He said to him, 'Go home to your people and report to them what great things the Lord has done for you, and how He had mercy on you.' And he went away and began to proclaim in Decapolis what great things Jesus had done for him; and everyone was amazed.'

2 Corinthians 10:3-5 (NASB)

"I ask that when I am present I need not be bold with the confidence with which I propose to be courageous against some, who regard us as if we walked according to the flesh. For though we walk in the flesh, we do not war according to the flesh, for the weapons of our warfare are not of the flesh, but divinely powerful for the destruction of fortresses. We are destroying speculations and every lofty thing raised up against the knowledge of God, and we are taking every thought captive to the obedience of Christ."

A STORY IS TOLD OF A MAN WHO WAS VISITING THE CIRCUS. When he arrived, he saw a big elephant held down by a very small chain. He approached the trainer and asked him, "How does that small chain hold such a large animal? The trainer replied, "It doesn't. But the elephant doesn't know that." The trainer explained to him that when the elephant was young and much smaller, a chain was placed on his ankle. It was strong enough to hold him because he was just a baby elephant. As he grew, they continued to use the same chain. When he became an adult, he was much stronger than the chain and could easily break it but he didn't try. The trainer then said, "It's not the chain that holds him down, it's the memory of the chain." Even though he is much bigger now, he is still living as though he hasn't changed. The elephant doesn't realize how strong he is now. He only remembers how weak he used to be, but the chains are still holding him back.

This is true. Chains will hold us back from becoming all that God intended us to be. You have likely heard the phrase that some people have a memory like an elephant. It means they don't forget anything. Tell them they can't do something they have never done before and they accept it. Tell them the chains of life will hold you back, so stop trying. It's useless. We respond in a similar fashion. In fact, I suspect that in one way or another, every one of us can identify with that story. It's a fact that many of us have chains that are holding us back and God has already given us the strength to break loose. Perhaps you were told as a child, "You'll never amount to anything," and the chains were put into place. "Why can't you be like your brother or your sister?" The chains were put into place. "You can't do anything right!" The chains were locked. Perhaps it wasn't your parents, maybe it was your so-called friends, and for some reason you were made to feel as though you never measured up to anyone else. The source doesn't really matter. What does matter is that you bought into a lie and that lie has held you in chains all of your life. Fortunately, there is a solution. God has given us a wonderful gift called grace and grace has the power to break those chains.

CHAINS CAN HOLD US BACK FROM BECOMING ALL GOD WANTS US TO BE.

This passage is recorded three times in the gospels. Matthew, Mark, and Luke all give us an account of this story. It's interesting that this story follows the story of when the disciples were out at sea and a storm came up and Jesus calmed the waters. It was after that when they approached land that they came to this place where there were tombs and caves. There they encountered a man who the Bible tells us was possessed by a demon. Mark tells us that the man had been suffering for a long time. Many people from the town had come to offer a variety of treatments, but nothing had helped. We then learn an interesting truth about the man. He was able to break free from the chains, but still was not able to move forward with his life. In his mind, the chains were still in place.

This reminds us that there are at least two kinds of chains that can hold us back. There are physical chains. The apostle Paul was placed in chains numerous times for sharing his faith. We believe that on at least four occasions while writing half of the New Testament, Paul was chained to a prison guard to keep him from escaping. Those were physical chains. This passage reminds us there are also mental and emotional chains that hold us back, which is what I am describing now. Mark paints a vivid picture of what this man's life was like. He was violent. No one could pass safely along the road where he lived. He was strong enough to break the chains but not strong enough to break the power of the demons. He was even violent toward himself and cut himself with stones. Self-cutting is a huge issue today. I see the fresh cuts on the arms and legs of people who cut themselves. I wonder what would cause someone to do something like that and inflict that kind of pain on themselves. I knew a teenager very well and she was cutting herself, so I asked her what would cause her to do that. This was her response. "Cutting, even though it causes pain, takes my mind off the greater pain I am experiencing at the time." I thought how terrible the other pain must be for her to do that, and there are thousands of young people doing it apparently for the same reason. Pain can cause us to do things we would not normally do. Pain can cause us to make decisions we would not normally make. It can turn people into addicts because they are willing to do anything to get rid of the greater pain. Verse 6 tells us that when the man saw Jesus, he ran to Him and fell on his knees in front of him to worship him. Clearly this was the right thing to do. When we bring ourselves before God in worship, there is power.

This man who was sick brought himself to a Place of Grace. He brought himself to Jesus.

In 1st John, the Bible tells us that the reason the Son of God appeared was to destroy the work of Satan. That is what He does here. What we have here is a picture of a wrestling match. Jesus against the forces of evil in this man. The demon suddenly acknowledged that he was in the presence of someone who was greater than he was. Philippians 2:10-11 tells us that, "At the feet of Jesus, every knee shall bow and every tongue confess that Jesus Christ is Lord." That is what is happening here. The demons were actually driving the man toward Jesus. In some way it seems the demons were attracted to His power or perhaps they thought they could defeat Jesus.

In Verse 9, Jesus commands the demon to identify himself. This was done to help bring healing to the man, so that he would then confess. Confession is powerful. Confession releases shame, breaks down walls, and tears chains apart. There is power when we confess. The Bible tells us in Romans that, "If you will confess with your mouth that Jesus is Lord and believe in your heart that you will be saved." His confession of who he is was, "I am legion." Legion basically means many. This man was being controlled by numerous evil forces and more than anything he needed the grace of Jesus in His life. In military terms, legion means six thousand. I'm not suggesting he had that many demons, but he did have an army of them and his life was miserable. One thing the demons knew for sure at this point was that the battle had been lost, so they begged Jesus not to send them back into the abyss. The abyss was the bottomless pit; back into Hell itself. They pleaded with Jesus to send them into a herd of pigs that were nearby instead. On the surface, this seems like a strange request. Demons had a way of causing great violence when they left someone. Perhaps the demons thought that since pigs were considered unclean anyway, Jesus might honor their request. The Great Physician Jesus is always concerned with bringing three things to an individual who is hurting:

1. To heal them.

2. To bring relief from pain.

3. To comfort them.

That is exactly what He does in this case. Jesus gives the man visible proof that his chains are gone. At that moment, the pigs ran down into the river and were drowned. The possessed man witnessed all of this and he knew that finally his chains were not only broken physically, they were also broken mentally. They were completely gone.

One thing we must take note of here is that the demons could not do anything without the permission of Jesus. They had to ask before they could move. Jesus was and still is superior to the evil forces in our world. The people tending to the animals were not the owners, but they must have known this was going to cause quite a reaction by the people in the area—a herd of two thousand pigs rushing down this river bank into the river. At that point, an even greater crowd appears and they are astonished. This man who was so sick in so many ways now sat before them, calm, dressed, and of sound mind. Not only that, he was sitting with Jesus. Their response was that they were afraid. They had one request of Jesus. Please let us get out of here. We're ready to leave. I wonder why. Were they worried because they had lost this entire herd of pigs, which was their income? Perhaps they were just afraid of the power of Jesus they had just witnessed. We don't know, but we do see that Jesus allowed them to leave.

Let's put our focus back where it belongs—on the man who had been demon possessed and an outcast from society. He was the only one besides Jesus who knew how the value of this gift he received. This man had one request also. "Jesus, can I go with you?" Do you blame him? Jesus declined. The man begged him. Still Jesus said no. He leaves him there as a witness to the powerful grace of Jesus Christ. Jesus told him to return to his family and said, "Tell everyone what God has done for you." The man did just that. Can you imagine the witness this man had to all who knew his past? This was the *Decapolis*. The Decapolis is an area composed of ten cities and everyone there was a Gentile. It had to start somewhere, and Jesus chose this man to do it. He was the first seed of what would become a mighty harvest. Amazing grace unchained him. Amazing grace set him free, not only physically, but spiritually and mentally. He was a new creation in Christ. Jesus has to start somewhere with someone. Why not you? Perhaps He has brought you to a Place of Grace so you can help others complete the journey also.

CHAPTER 15:

Pick Up Your Towel

"Please, for the love of God, pick up your towels."

—Every Mother

John 13:1-17 (NASB)

"Now before the Feast of the Passover, Jesus knowing that His hour had come that He would depart out of this world to the Father, having loved His own who were in the world, He loved them to the end. During supper, the devil having already put into the heart of Judas Iscariot, the son of Simon, to betray Him, Jesus, knowing that the Father had given all things into His hands, and that He had come forth from God and was going back to God, got up from supper, and laid aside His garments; and taking a towel, He girded Himself. Then He poured water into the basin, and began to wash the disciples' feet and to wipe them with the towel with which He was girded. So He came to Simon Peter. He said to Him, 'Lord, do You wash my feet?' Jesus answered and said to him, 'What I do you do not realize now, but you will understand here-after.' Peter said to Him, 'Never shall You wash my feet!' Jesus answered him, 'If I do not wash you, you have no part with Me.' Simon Peter said to Him, 'Lord, then wash not only my feet, but also my hands and my head.' Jesus said to him, 'He who has bathed needs only to wash his feet, but is completely clean; and you are clean, but not all of you.' For He knew the one who was betraying Him; for this reason He said, 'Not all of you are clean.' So when He had washed their feet, and taken His garments and reclined at the table again, He said to them, 'Do you know what I have done to you? You call Me Teacher and Lord; and you are right, for so I am. If I then, the Lord and the Teacher, washed your feet, you also ought to wash one another's feet. For I gave you an example that you also should do as I did to you. Truly, truly, I say to you, a slave is not greater than his master, nor is one who is sent greater than the one who sent him. If you know these things, you are blessed if you do them.'"

THERE ARE MANY DIFFERENT NAMES/TITLES GIVEN TO JESUS in Scripture. Words like, "Advocate." He is like a lawyer defending us. With words like "Alpha" and "Omega," he is telling us he is the beginning and the end. One of my favorites is that he was called, "Friend of sinners." There are dozens of different titles Jesus had, but one title we never see is "Hypocrite."

Jesus made very sure that his words and his actions were always in sync. Always. When he taught something, he also lived it out. In fact, he would always go the extra mile to make his point. In the Sermon on the Mount, he said if someone sues you and wants your shirt, let them have your coat too. If a soldier demands that you carry his gear for a mile, carry it two miles. If someone slaps you on the right cheek, offer the other cheek also. In each of these cases, you have someone who is not exactly your friend, but is demanding something from you. A man sues you and now you not only give him what he wants, you give him more than what he asked. A soldier orders you to carry his gear for a mile and you say, "Sure I'll carry it two miles." Someone hits you and you say, "Hit me again, I like it." Who does that? I'll tell you who—Jesus—and He expects the same from us. In this passage, we learn that Jesus had begun to recognize that his time had come. It was time for him to leave this world and return to his father. Jesus knew exactly who he was and he knew exactly what he was supposed to do. His purpose was clear. At one point, Jesus said, "I have come to seek and to save that which was lost."[34] We talk many times about what it means to find ourselves—our true selves—and to know who we really are. There is really not much more important than understanding our real identity in Jesus Christ. This is when we discover our purpose, meaning, and direction in life. You were made on purpose, FOR a purpose. Jesus knew exactly who he was and what he was supposed to do.

Jesus knew the source of His power and He knew the source of his life. Too many times we underestimate what God can do in our lives and we overestimate what we can do. We think, "I've got this God. I can do this." If our pride swells too much, then we begin to think, "Hey, maybe I can even do this without him." That is the ultimate mistake. That is the ultimate sin. The sin of pride.

In the prophecy of Isaiah, the writer reminds us of the words of Lucifer himself before his fall. Read Isaiah 14:13-14. This is what Lucifer did. He underestimated God and he overestimated himself. The result of that is seen in Verse 15. The apostle Paul had it exactly right in the scripture when he said, "I can do all things through Christ who gives me strength."[35]

This is what I see in this passage. There is no limit to what you and I can do as long as we understand from where our strength comes. Once pride steps in, we are done. Once pride steps out, God will use us. Take a look at your pride. Jesus knows who He was and what He was supposed to do. Jesus knows the source of His power. He knows the source of life. Now he acts on what he knows. Look at verses 4-5. What did Jesus do with all the knowledge and power he carried around? He

JESUS WAS THE CEO OF FOOTWASHERS, INC. AND HE IS ALWAYS LOOKING FOR EMPLOYEES.

washed feet. He was the CEO of Footwashers, Inc. He was always looking for employees by the way. He offered a lot of benefits—the best fire insurance policy you can have, if you know what I mean. You just have to bring one thing with you to work each day—a towel. A towel is a symbol of servanthood. This is who we are—servants. The Greek word is *doulos*, which actually means slave. Jesus was always willing to go the extra mile when necessary. He hung out with sinners, he healed the sick, he fed the hungry, and he touched the leper. Jesus always went the second mile and he challenges us to do the same.

In 2000, my wife and I planted a new church in the Tampa Bay area in Florida. Prior to doing so, I attended a three-day seminar sponsored by the North American Mission Board. There were approximately one hundred pastors in attendance. All of us came with an abundance of questions, hoping to figure out how to start this new venture. For me, I not only came with questions, I was also a bit burned out due to conflict in the church and had thoughts of just throwing in the towel. The meeting, however, was excellent. I became excited about the possibilities of planting a brand new church in our area. On the final evening the speaker said, "I am going to pick three of you to help lead the worship service tonight." He looked around the room and pointing his finger he said, "I'll take you and you and you." One of those he selected was me. I had no idea why. He then closed the session with prayer and we took a break for dinner. My first thought was, "What does he want me to do?" When the session ended, I went to him and inquired, "Is there anything I need to do to prepare for tonight?" He said, "No, not a thing. Just bring a towel with you." I was puzzled, but I thought, "Well, that's simple enough."

I returned to the evening session with my towel in hand, still puzzled as to what we would be doing. He preached a great closing message and then asked for the three of us to come to the front with our towels. He announced that the three of us would now get on our knees and crawl from aisle to aisle and shine the shoes of everyone present. I kept my shoes shined. I often shined my kid's shoes, but I had never shined the shoes of someone I hardly knew—especially that many. The three of us proceeded to our assignment—crawling through each row, shining the shoes of about thirty-five pastors apiece. It was humbling, but at the same time it felt strangely encouraging. God was showing me what it meant to truly serve. Somewhere on my journey that evening from row to row, on hands and knees, shining shoes, God spoke to me and said, "Next time you feel like throwing in the towel, instead, pick it up and serve me." It was clear to me God was not finished with me and I sensed his amazing grace coming over me as I served. He was moving me to a new place—a place of grace.

CHAPTER 16:

Dealing with Emptiness

"The emptiness of the cup is its usefulness."

—BRUCE LEE

John 20:1-29 (NASB)

"Now on the first day of the week Mary Magdalene came early to the tomb, while it was still dark, and saw the stone already taken away from the tomb. So she ran and came to Simon Peter and to the other disciple whom Jesus loved, and said to them, 'They have taken away the Lord out of the tomb, and we do not know where they have laid Him.' So Peter and the other disciple went forth, and they were going to the tomb. The two were running together; and the other disciple ran ahead faster than Peter and came to the tomb first; and stooping and looking in, he saw the linen wrappings lying there; but he did not go in. And so Simon Peter also came, following him, and entered the tomb; and he saw the linen wrappings lying there, and the face-cloth which had been on His head, not lying with the linen wrappings, but rolled up in a place by itself. So the other disciple who had first come to the tomb then also entered, and he saw and believed. For as yet they did not understand the Scripture; that He must rise again from the dead. So the disciples went away again to their own homes. But Mary was standing outside the tomb weeping; and so, as she wept, she stooped and looked into the tomb; and she saw two angels in white sitting, one at the head and one at the feet, where the body of Jesus had been lying. And they said to her, 'Woman, why are you weeping?' She said to them, 'Because they have taken away my Lord, and I do not know where they have laid Him.' When she had said this, she turned around and saw Jesus standing there, and did not know that it was Jesus. Jesus said to her, 'Woman, why are you weeping? Whom are you seeking?' Supposing Him to be the gardener, she said to Him, 'Sir, if you have carried Him away, tell me where you have laid Him, and I will take Him away.' Jesus said to her, 'Mary!' She turned and said to Him in Hebrew, 'Rabboni!' (which means, Teacher). Jesus said to her, 'Stop clinging to Me, for I have not yet ascended to the Father; but go to My brethren and say to them, 'I ascend to My Father and your Father, and My God and your God.'' Mary Magdalene came, announcing to the disciples, 'I have seen the Lord,' and that He had said these things to her. So when it was evening on that day, the first day of the week, and when the doors were shut where the disciples were, for fear of the Jews, Jesus came and stood in their midst and said to them, 'Peace be with you.' And when He had said this, He showed them both His hands and His side. The disciples then rejoiced when they saw the Lord. So Jesus said to them again, 'Peace be with you; as the Father has sent Me, I also send you.' And when He had said this, He breathed on them and said to them, 'Receive the Holy Spirit. If you forgive the sins of any, their sins have been forgiven them; if you retain the sins of any, they have been retained.' But Thomas, one of the twelve, called Didymus, was not with them when Jesus came. So the other disciples were saying to him, 'We have seen the Lord!' But he said to them, 'Unless I see in His hands the imprint of the nails, and put my finger into the place of the nails, and put my hand into His side, I will not believe.' After eight days His disciples were again inside, and Thomas with them. Jesus came, the doors having been shut, and stood in their midst and said, 'Peace be with you.' Then He said to Thomas, 'Reach here with your finger, and see My hands; and reach here your hand and put it into My side; and do not be unbelieving, but believing.' Thomas answered and said to Him, 'My Lord and my God!' Jesus said to him, 'Because you have seen Me, have you believed? Blessed are they who did not see, and yet believed.'"

DR. BILLY GRAHAM SHARED THE STORY OF HOW HE LEARNED to preach by going to a local lake and standing on the bank and preaching to the alligators. Many pastors actually practice their messages before they preach them. Hearing it out loud helps you realize how you are going to sound to the group you are speaking to. During the COVID-19 pandemic, I preached to an empty building for four months so that our congregation could view the service online. It's very different and I also learned a lot by doing it. I really missed seeing the expressions on people's faces as I preach. I missed the occasional "Amen" someone would say, and most of all I missed the interaction with the people because preaching to an empty building kind of makes you feel empty as well. It's just not the same.

When we look at the word empty or emptiness in the dictionary we find these definitions:

- Emptiness means to lack meaning.

- Emptiness means to be insincere.

- Emptiness means to lack value or purpose in life.

- When Job spoke in the Old Testament, the Bible tells us that for a time his words were empty. They had no meaning.

- God speaks through the prophet Isaiah and says, "So is my word that goes out from my mouth: it will not return to me empty."[36] In other words, there is nothing empty about God's voice and His words.

From the beginning of scripture, we find out about emptiness because the writer of Genesis tells us from the beginning of time, "In the beginning God created the heavens and the earth. Now the earth was formless and empty."[37] At one time or another, every one of us has felt empty. Life seems to have lost its meaning and we seem to have lost our purpose. However, emptiness doesn't have to always put us in a bad place. Emptiness can actually be a Place of Grace.

In John 20, we find the story of the resurrection. It is the crowning achievement of Jesus, even greater than the cross. Now read this carefully. Without the resurrection, the cross would have no meaning. Our Savior would be dead. Because of the resurrection, we can even in our emptiness proclaim that the tomb is empty because we serve a risen Savior. On the day we know as Good Friday, Jesus had already been arrested, had experienced what was perhaps the most unfair trial in history, and was sentenced to death on a cross early

EMPTINESS CAN ACTUALLY BE A PLACE OF GRACE.

that morning. Those six hours he spent, from 9AM until 3PM, are best described as torture. He had already received the dreaded thirty-nine lashes where an individual would be beaten within an inch of his life. They spit in His face and punched Him with their fists. Soldiers gambled for his robe and then made a crown of thorns, forcing it down on His forehead to mock Him as King of the Jews. No man has ever received more torture and punishment than Jesus. On top of the physical pain He experienced, He also went through great spiritual pain. The sin of all mankind was placed on Him that day as he died to offer salvation to a lost world. He spoke seven different times from that cross on that Friday saying things such as:

- "Father forgive them, for they know not what they are doing." That is the ultimate form of forgiveness.

- He said to the thief on the cross, who have His life over to Jesus, "Today you will be with me in paradise."

- He said, "I thirst." This was his humanity coming out.

- Then He speaks a phrase out of complete feelings of emptiness as He spoke to the Father these words, "My God, My God, why have you forsaken me?" To me that is the ultimate statement of emptiness when we says God, my friends and family have left me, I feel alone and NOW you have left me. I feel completely empty.

Just to clarify, we believe the reason Jesus spoke those words was because a Holy God could not look upon the sins of the world that all been cast upon Jesus. There is no way that you and I can fathom how empty Jesus felt at this moment.

Now it is the first day of the week, and while it's still dark, Mary Magdalene went to the tomb and saw that the stone had been removed. Her first response was, "They have taken my Lord and I don't know where they have put Him."[38] We then learn that Peter and the other disciples raced to get to the tomb. The other one we know is John. John apparently ran track in high school, because he outruns Peter and gets to the tomb first and looks inside. He didn't actually step into the tomb, but he does recognize at this point that the tomb is empty. He saw the strips of linen which were the clothes Jesus was buried in, and the cloth that had been wrapped around the head of Jesus. John then tells us that the cloth was still lying in place, but was separate from the linen. John and Peter both then step inside the tomb and the scripture simply tells us, "They believed." John also tells us that they still did not understand that Jesus had to rise from the dead. Then they went back to where they were staying. At this point, they still did not understand completely that a resurrection had taken place. Instead they must have felt very, very empty. How could someone steal the body of Jesus?

We then learn that Mary Magdalene was standing outside the tomb crying. She felt empty also. She bent over and peeked into the tomb, seeing the linen cloths. She also saw two angels, dressed in white and they were seated where Jesus had been—one at the head of the slab and one at the foot. The angels asked her why she was crying and Mary replied, "They have taken my Lord away and I don't know here they have put Him." She then turned around and standing there was a man she believed to be the gardener, who took care of the cemetery, but it was actually Jesus. Jesus spoke to her and asked, "Who is it you are looking for?" She says, "Well, sir if you have carried Him away, tell me where you have put Him and I will get Him."[39] Jesus then says her name—"Mary." She then recognized His voice, realized this was her Savior, and turned and cried out to Him, "Teacher!" Jesus warned her not to touch Him. Mary immediately ran away and went to the disciples with the best news we could ever hear. "I have just seen Jesus! He's alive!" I can only imagine that at that moment her emptiness began to fade.

- Her life had meaning and purpose again.

- She had a reason to hope.

- She had a reason to move forward.

- She had a reason now to spread the good news.

That is exactly what she does. She ran to tell all of the disciples. That evening, all of the disciples gathered together in one house and locked the doors. I am sure they were afraid for their lives because Jesus was missing from the tomb. Out of the blue, with the doors locked, Jesus appeared to them, showed them the nail prints in his wrists and the scar in His side and said, "Peace be with you!" Then He breathed on them and said, "Receive the Holy Spirit." He closed the conversation by talking to them about the importance for forgiveness. Jesus appeared to Thomas because he was not present with the rest of the disciples, and Thomas said, "I need to touch the wounds in his wrist and the scar in his side before I will believe." He does and then he proclaims, "My Lord and my God."[40]

Emptiness is not a feeling we enjoy, but when it comes to the tomb of Jesus, I have different thoughts. Can you imagine what it must have been like when Peter, John, and Mary Magdalene peeked into the tomb and it was empty? The tomb was empty because Jesus was not there.

BECAUSE OF AN EMPTY TOMB, OUR HEARTS CAN BE FULL.

The greatest miracle in history had occurred, all because of emptiness. This empty tomb meant one thing—Our Savior was alive! Old Testament prophecies were fulfilled in a matter of moments. A bodily resurrection from the dead had taken place just as Jesus had promised. Who would have thought that emptiness could be just a beautiful thing! The tomb was empty. As a result, our hearts don't have to feel empty. Jesus arose from the dead so that our hearts can be filled with Jesus.

An old hymn says it best. "You ask me how I know He lives. He lives within my heart!"[41] You can know all about Him today in your head. You can possess tremendous head knowledge. From the top of the brain to the heart is about sixteen inches. My point is that you can know about Jesus, but if you don't have Him in your heart, you will miss Heaven by sixteen inches. It's not about knowledge and it's not about trying to earn it. It's about a relationship with our Savior Jesus Christ. He is our Place of Grace.

CHAPTER 17:

Why Do Very Bad Things Happen to Very Good People?

"That only happened once and He volunteered."

—R.C. SPROUL

THIS IS A QUESTION THAT IS ASKED PERHAPS MORE THAN ANY other question about God. It is a question people around the world are asking right at this moment. It has been referred to as "The Achilles Heel of Christianity"—the question that often keeps people from becoming believers in Christ. If you could ask God one question, what would it be? The top response from most people is this. "Why is there pain and suffering in the world. Why do bad things happen to good people? C.S. Lewis in his book *The Problem of Pain* says the problem with pain is that pain requires attention. Pain insists on being attended to.[42]

We ask these kinds of questions, not for the purpose of some sort of intellectual debate. We ask questions like these because they affect all of us on a very personal level. These kinds of questions can either make us or break us. They can make us bitter or they can make us better. You and I are the ones who must decide how we will allow tragedy and pain to affect us.

To get an answer to this question we turn to the Book of James. James is one of the most practical books in the New Testament. James is not a book of deep doctrine. It is not an explanation of how to be saved. James is a letter written to believers who already knew the basics of the Christian faith and his intention was to drive home the importance of living out the truth. This book was written to us to help us mature in the faith. The main issue that prompted James to write is still a concern today. If you say you believe, then why do you live as though you don't?

James begins by identifying himself simply as James, a servant of God and the Lord Jesus Christ. We believe this is James, the brother of Jesus—one of four sons born to Joseph and Mary. I grew up with three brothers and one sister. If you have a large family, parents can often compare one child to another. "Why can't you be more like your brother?" Can you imagine growing up in a home where your brother was Jesus? How do you think it felt to literally have a perfect brother? James, why can't you be more like Jesus? Perhaps this makes it easier to understand why James did not believe until after the resurrection. He did not grow up as a believer.[43] Not only did James then come to faith, he was also declared an apostle and it is commonly thought that he pastored the church in Jerusalem. He was known for his profound prayer life. In fact his nickname was "Old camel knees" because of callouses on his knees from praying.[44]

James is writing to a group of Jewish believers who were undergoing severe hardship. They were hated—despised—because they were Jews. James could pat them all on the back and comfort them, but instead he challenged them. He told them to put on your big boy pants because you've got to learn to trust God when things go bad. Grow up! In many churches today many preach that the Christian life will always keep you healthy. You will be wealthy, and life will always be good. You will always be healthy, wealthy, and wise. James would have laughed at those sermons. That kind of preaching would be a foreign concept to James. James never taught that becoming a believer would suddenly make all of your problems disappear and that you would live happily ever after. C.S. Lewis said that, "We want, in fact, not so much a father in heaven; a senile benevolence who, as they say, 'liked to see young people enjoying themselves' and whose plan for the universe was simply that it might be truly said at the end of each day, 'A good time was had by all." Most of us don't want a Father in heaven – we want a grandfather in heaven."[45] Grandparents are the ones who make everything all right. They can spoil the kids and then send them home to their parents.

All of us face trials. It is our tendency to ask how to avoid these trials or make them go away. The real question should be, "How can I change the way I respond to hard times?"

First of all, it helps to realize that difficulties come into everyone's life. Verse 2 tells us, "Consider it joy when you fall into trials." James is telling us that bad things are not optional—they are inevitable. He does not say IF you encounter bad things; he says WHEN you encounter them. There is an interesting word James uses here in the Greek—it means varied. It is the word for our English term, "polka dot." It is not the idea that we are going to have many trials; it is the idea that we are going to have all kinds of them—varied kinds.

- Loss of a job

- Broken relationships

- Illness that lingers

- A wayward child

- Depression that lingers

- Even a pandemic

Whatever those trials might be, they can be overwhelming. James says, basically if you are a believer, people will know it based on how you respond to trials. If your faith is only good when things are good, then you don't need it. If your faith is only good when you're doing well, then you don't really need it. True faith sustains us when everything goes wrong. Difficulties will come into everyone's life.

Next, it is your attitude that determines the outcome. Again in Verse 2, we learn that most of us, when we face some trial—some bad thing that is happening—will ultimately ask, "Why?' Why am I going through this? What purpose could this possibly serve? I know I have heard that question too many times. However, let me ask you. Have you ever really searched for the answer to that question? It's easier to just throw up your arms in disgust, blame God, and say, "I'm done!" The reason for that is our attitude, which can be:

- Angry

- Disgusted

- Bitter

- Frustrated

Look again at Verse 2 and notice the word "count." "Count it joy when you fall into trials. Count is an accounting term which means to "evaluate" or to "add up." James hits right at the heart of our problem. The heart of the human problem is the problem of the human heart. It is our attitude. James is saying if we are going to benefit from our trials, not just wade through them but actually benefit from them, then we must deal with our attitude. He is not saying that trials are a joy to go through. He is saying we should COUNT them, evaluate them, and don't ignore them. Don't go into denial and act as though they never happened. Look clearly at them.

Remember what CS Lewis said—pain requires our attention. Pain insists on being tended to. For many of us, some things keep happening over and over because we don't pay any attention to them. We just wait for them to end, and that is the wrong approach.

In Philip Yancey's book, *Where is God When it Hurts?* he puts it this way. "Rejoicing in suffering does not mean we should be happy about tragedy and pain when we really feel like crying or falling apart. The Bible focuses on the end-result; how God can use the suffering in our lives. But before He can use it He needs us to trust Him." Yancey then says that the process of giving him that commitment can be described as rejoicing.[46]

ATTITUDE DETERMINES OUTCOME. ATTITUDE IS EVERYTHING.

We can be absolutely certain God has a purpose in our trials. From Verses 3 and 4, we know that trials have a purpose and can make a big difference in how we face these bad times. No matter how you might feel, God has not abandoned you. He has not in the past, nor will He in the future. Peter tells us in his first letter, "May the thought of this cause you to jump for joy, even though lately you've had to put up with the grief of many trials."[47] According to James, enduring these bad things produces certain characteristics in those who are going through them. Like the saying or song tells us, "What doesn't kill us makes us stronger."[48]

Look at this:

- We will become perfect. The word there means mature or fit for a purpose. It does not mean sinless.

- We will become complete. Whole. Fully developed.

- We will be lacking in nothing. God will provide everything we need to remain obedient during the bad times.

James isn't just suggesting that we count trials as joyful. He is commanding us to do so—to allow this way of thinking to completely control our minds and our actions. It is a command that he gives us. Understand this. If I said, "Raise your hand into the air," that is something you can actually do. You can "will" your hand to rise into the air. However if I said, "Jump up and touch the moon," well that is something that you cannot do. That is a command you are not capable of following. THIS command is one that is possible. Here is the catch. You have to be the one to do it. No one else can do it for you. You have to make a decision to do it. You can learn to count your trials as joy. God has a purpose in our good times as well as our bad times. We were not intended to go through these bad times alone. We read in verse 5 through 8 that believers do not go through trials alone. We have wisdom at our disposal. It's not automatic. We must ask. We need insight on how to go through these bad things. Wisdom is applied knowledge. It is when we put knowledge to use. We know what these verses say to do (verses 2-4), but the question is how do we put them into practice? Do we stay where we are? Do we move? How should we respond? James says, simple, ask God and He will let you know what to do.

God intends for our trials to become blessings (Verse 12). Blessed is a beatitude, like Matthew Chapter 5. Blessed means happy and to be satisfied. Joy is contentment even when trials come our way. Too many times, we see people come to Christ. They are then baptized but before long, they go back to their old way of life. Trouble comes along and they are gone. They may never come back. They shook their fist at God and that was it. When golf balls were first manufactured, they made the covers smooth. Then they discovered that after a ball had been roughed up, you could get more distance out of it, so they started manufacturing them with dimpled covers. It is this way with life as well. It takes some rough spots to make us go the farthest. Keep your focus where it belongs—on Jesus—because this trial you are going through can actually become a place of grace.

During World War II, Anne Frank received a diary for her thirteenth birthday. Just one month later, she was forced into hiding with her family and basically spent the next part of her life a small house, in an attic and not being able go outside. She was literally in fear for her life. She kept a diary and it is published now. She journaled her thoughts. She lived in a secret attic apartment for two years, over seven hundred days. On days that the enemy came into her small house she said, "Whenever someone comes in from outside, with the wind in their clothes and the cold on their cheeks, I feel like burying my head under the blankets to keep from thinking, 'When will we be allowed to breathe fresh air again?' I long to ride a bike, to dance, to whistle, to look at the world, feel young and know that I'm free, and yet I can't let it show."[49]

Her position in life was far worse than what we face, yet she persevered. She chose life each day over worry. She chose to look to the future rather than dwell on the moment. We must learn to think as Jesus would think. This is not the time to shrink back in fear. It is the time to rise up and make a difference. People are watching to see what the church will do. This is our time—our time to show the world just how real Jesus is. It is time for all of us to become A Place of Grace.

EPILOGUE

Early in the twentieth century, Joseph Stalin was General Secretary of the Communist Party in Russia. Did you know that in his early days he went to seminary, planning to become a priest? Obviously his direction in life changed. During his time as President of the Communist Party, forty two thousand priests lost their lives. The total number of priests went from three hundred eighty thousand to one hundred seventy-two. A thousand monasteries, sixty seminaries, and ninety-eight out of every one hundred Orthodox churches were closed. A film has been made describing all of this, called *Repentance*. In one scene in the movie, women living in a small village gathered in a muddy river to inspect logs as they floated down the river. What were they doing? They were hoping to find a message carved in one of the logs from their husbands who were working in the prison camps cutting these logs. They were desperate for a word from them to learn that they were still alive. One woman found initials carved into the bark of the log. She began weeping loudly and hugging the tree because it was the closest connection she had to her husband. The movie ends with a peasant woman asking someone on the street for directions to a church. She is told she is on the wrong street. She replies, "What good is a street if it doesn't lead to a church?"[50] What good is a path if it doesn't lead to Jesus? I would ask, "What good is a path that doesn't lead to a Place of Grace?"

ENDNOTES

Chapter 1

1 John 21:25 NASB

2 John 1:29 ESV

3 Leviticus 17:11 NASB

4 John 2:4 NASB

Chapter 2

5 James 1:17 NASB

6 Psalm 46:10 NIV

7 Glenn Turner Quotes. BrainyQuote.com, BrainyMedia Inc, 2020. https://www.brainyquote.com/quotes/glenn_turner_108587, accessed May 1, 2020.

8 Insights for Living. Dr. Chuck Swindoll. The Value of a Positive Attitude. November 19, 1995.

9 https://jwbrooksblog.wordpress.com/2014/11/10

10 https://joemckeever.com/wp/the-best-article-ever. January 4, 2010.

Chapter 3

11 http://best-hoaxes.blogspot.com/2009/07

12 Romans 7:15-24 NIV

13 2nd Timothy 2:26 NIV

14 Romans 12:1-2 KJV

15 Stated in an interview with Dr. James Dobson. January 23, 1989.

16 Christianity Today. Coming Clean: An interview with Max Lucado. 2012

17 Romans 8:13 CSB

18 Lee Strobel, "Meet the Jesus I Know," Preaching Today. Audio #211

Chapter 4

19 Galatians 4:4-5

20 Soren Kierkegaard, "Philosophical Fragments," 1844, pages 31-42.

Chapter 5

21 William Barclay. The Gospel of John. Volume 2. Page 43.

22 Galatians 3:24. NIV

23 International Conference of Creativity, Thinking and Education, presented, 2015 at University of St. Thomas in Minnesota.

Chapter 6

24 "Living the Psalms: Encouragement for the Daily Grind." Chuck Swindoll, 2012. Psalm 32. Day 3. Worthy Books.

Chapter 7

25   https://www.forbes.com/sites/laurabegleybloom/2019

Chapter 8

26   Matthew 12:38-42 NASB

Chapter 10

27   40 Days by Alton Gransky. Published by Broadman & Holman. 2007

Chapter 11

28   Your God is too Small by J. B. Phillips. Publisher: Touchstone; Reprint edition (May 1, 1997).

Chapter 12

29   No Little People, copyright 1974; The Complete Works of Francis Schaeffer, vol. 3, 1982.

30   Holman New Christian Commentary, Max Anders, General editor. Volume 8, pages 152-157.

31   Ibid.

Chapter 13

32   WebMd.com. Reviewed by Jennifer Robinson, MD. December 10, 2017.

33   2 Chronicles 7:14 NKJV

Chapter 15

34   Matthew 18:11. NASB.

35   Philippians 4:13. NIV

Chapter 16

36 Isaiah 55:11 NIV

37 Genesis 1:2 NIV

38 John 20:13 NLT

39 John 20:15 NLT

40 John 20:28 NLT

41 He Lives. Written by A.F. Meyers. 19th century.

Chapter 17

42 The Problem of Pain by C.S. Lewis. Page 57.

43 John 7:5 NIV

44 The Apostle-A Life of Paul. John Pollock. 1969. Page 85.

45 https://www.cslewisinstitute.org/God_is_Love

46 Philip Yancey, Where Is God When It Hurts? (Grand Rapids: Zondervan, 1990), Kindle Locations 1697-1702

47 The Passion Translation. Copyright 2017 by Passion & Fire Ministries, Inc.

48 https://www.brainyquote.com/quotes/friedrich_nietzsche

49 The Diary of Anne Frank. Contact Publishing. 1946.

50 What's so amazing about Grace? Philip Yancey. Zondervan. Page 128